A Life Well Lived:

The Jennifer Paulson Story

By

Eric Lundberg

With a special Foreword by
Jennifer's Mother and Father

authorHOUSE®

AuthorHouse™
1663 Liberty Drive
Bloomington, IN 47403
www.authorhouse.com
Phone: 1-800-839-8640

First published by AuthorHouse   02/28/2011

ISBN: 978-1-4567-3606-4 (hc)
ISBN: 978-1-4567-3607-1 (e)
ISBN: 978-1-4567-3608-8 (sc)

Printed in the United States of America

The dedication of this book is divided three ways:

First and foremost I dedicate this book to Ned and Nancy, Ken and Cindy, Mark, Becky, Savannah, and to Jason. May you be comforted by the enduring hope that you will be reunited with your Jennifer again soon and you will walk together on streets of gold, as if no time has passed at all.

Secondly, to every student Ms. Paulson ever taught. I pray that you will always know how proud of you she is and that you will find the value and potential in yourself that she did.

And finally, to you, dear reader, that through these pages you will learn to believe in the living God that drove Jennifer to a life well lived.

Contents

Special Foreword by
Nancy Heisler

When I became pregnant with Jennifer, I never dreamed I would have a girl. At the time the Paulson family was made up of all boys, with just one girl. Jennifer's father was the youngest of five boys and as for me I had three older brothers and no sisters. So I think you can understand when I say: "I wanted a girl very much."

I was sick the whole nine months of my pregnancy. I remember when we went on a road trip with some friends of ours: Ralph and Margaret Lundberg. Ralph thought it was quite amusing when he would have to pull the van over along the side of the road so I could throw up. He would watch me in his side view mirror!

Jennifer Ann Paulson arrived June 23, 1979. I had an emergency C-Section and was put to sleep. Later that evening I was alert enough to know that God had blessed us with a healthy and beautiful baby girl. What a surprise! And she looked just like her dad.

Jennifer was a very good baby and a wonderful little girl. She was very easy going and never gave us any trouble. Her grandparents, Cliff and Selma Paulson, absolutely adored her. They were both so happy that we had a little girl and she had Grandpa Cliff wrapped around her little finger. When we would pick her up from Sunday school class at church she would run up to Grandpa and dive her little hands into his coat pocket searching for candy he would keep for her. When we visited their home, Grandpa would always set her on his kitchen counter so she could watch him make those wonderful strawberry milkshakes she loved so much.

Jennifer loved her friends and family so much and it was very important to her to spend time with both. She had the same friends from grade school through her short adult life. Her very first little friend was Eric Lundberg. They were friends from babies, and remained friends throughout her life. I have so many pictures and fond memories of the two of them. I would like to say thank you to all of Jennifer's friends who loved, supported and accepted her just the way she was.

Jennifer did well in school and excelled in everything that she did. After high school she went on to college to pursue a career in special education. After graduation she went to work for the Tacoma Public School

District. She later went back to school to pursue her Master's Degree and achieved in 2009. Jennifer developed into an excellent teacher and won the admiration and respect of many of her co-workers. She loved and cared for her students, and they could see the love of Jesus shine through her. She had asked me to pray with her on several occasions about one of her students. Her students had many wonderful things to say about her.

Jennifer loved the Lord and had a smile that lit up the entire room. She just wanted to love and serve Jesus for the rest of her life (and she did). I had a conversation with one of her friends after her death. Jennifer and Joellen had long, in-depth talks about death before Jennifer passed. They asked each other if they would be willing to die for Jesus. They both answered: *"Yes, I'm sure."* My Jennifer never thought she would be going to see the Lord so soon after that conversation.

Jennifer and I had some tough years. Her father and I divorced in December of 1995. She was only sixteen years old and this left her hurt, confused, and very angry. She went to live with her dad and we both missed out on a lot of time together. With the help of family, friends and, of course, God, she came through without any rebellious crazy stunts. I would like to thank God for guiding her life. I would like to thank Ken for being a kind, loving and gentle dad for her. Thank you for putting her first when I wasn't always able to.

As time went on and with God's help, Jennifer was able to forgive me and the healing began. I was remarried to Ned Heisler. He had four sons (a blended family...YEAH!) Jennifer once again had another bump in the road of her life to get through. With God's help once again she came though it. I don't want to make it sound like it was easy for her to overcome the hurts of her past, because it wasn't. The last few months of her life she was doing a Bible Study called *"Breaking Free"*, by Beth Moore. It focused on overcoming the hurts and disappointments in your life. After her death I read the study book she had been writing in, from the beginning to where she had stopped. I cried as I read it seeing how it was transforming her. Unfortunately, she was never able to finish the study. She always highly recommended the study saying it was the best one she had ever done- and always tried to get me to do it too. She was never able to live out the life changing principals she learned from it.

I used to say: *"My Jennifer is a rose among six thorns;"* the six thorns being her two brothers and four step brothers. Having her was the only thing that kept my sanity. I felt so sorry for her at family gatherings that she had to put up with six guys. As time went on things got better, some of the boys married and there were more girls. But now my rose is gone.

Ned and Jennifer grew to care for one another. They had many conversations about religion and politics. She was also a bit of a hypochondriac. She would call Ned, who is a firefighter and EMT, if she felt something wasn't quite right with her (thinking she was having a heart attack or something). He would listen to her symptoms and calmly reassure her that she was fine. Ned did so much for her. He mowed and weeded her lawn in the summer, he would fix things around her house, if there was anything she needed he would be there.

When her little brother Jason was around three or four years of age (Jennifer would have been eleven or twelve), she and a few of her friends dressed Jason up in some girl's clothes. He was so cute and all of them, including Jason, were having a great time (I have pictures and he was such a ham!) Jason is not going to appreciate me telling this story, but he would often times (while growing up) put his arms around Jennifer and hold so tight she couldn't move. Jennifer would say: *"Mom, make Jason let me go."* I would tell him to let her go and be nice to her. It was his way of teasing his big sister and showing her a little love; now he doesn't have her to hold onto anymore. Jennifer spent many hours helping him with his college papers. She would say to me: *"Look how far Jason has come."* Out of all of the family, she was the most excited to fly down to Texas to see him graduate. She was never able to; she died two months before his graduation.

Jennifer drove an older Chevrolet Lumina. It wasn't the most attractive looking car and she always seemed to be bumping into others or others seemed to be bumping into her. We always labeled her cars disposable. When she first got her license, I was afraid to ride with her. She had, however, improved over the years. For the last two years of her life, the heater and air conditioner quit working. She had to constantly refill her radiator; she couldn't defrost her windows or even heat her car. She drove around in the freezing winter, unable to see through her windshield (not so safe). During the hottest days of 2009 and no A/C, she said she felt like she couldn't breathe in the car. Everyone told her to get rid of the thing because it wasn't safe. She said: *"I know I should, but maybe I can make it just a little longer."* A few months before she died, she called me to say she thought God had healed her car. The heater suddenly started working again and she didn't need to add as much water. That was my Jennifer, she prayed for everything. She truly was a woman of God. Did I really give birth to this amazing young woman?

On the morning of February 26, 2010, my life changed forever. My beautiful daughter with a heart of gold and a never-ending smile died. The man that was stalking her went onto the grounds of the school where she worked, shot her and ended her life here on earth. I did not only loose my daughter that day, but also my best friend. I lost any future hopes and dreams. She will never again have the opportunity to fall in love, marry or have children. I will never get to help her plan her wedding and her dad will never get to walk her down the isle. There will be no more holidays, birthdays, vacations, camping trips, Bible studies, family gatherings, shopping, going out to lunch, cooking together, phone calls, talks, hugs or meeting her at church. No more anything-until we meet together in heaven.

Her brother Mark not only lost his sister but his friend. They are only twenty-five months apart. Her little brother Jason who is just twenty-three years old was just beginning to realize that his sister was more than a sister, but she could also be his friend. Now he will never get the opportunity to develop that adult brother and sister relationship. Her young niece, Savannah, will never have the opportunity to spend time with her Aunt Jennifer. When she is old enough I will show her pictures and tell her all about her aunt. He brothers will never have the opportunity to have holiday gatherings at Jennifer's house when their dad and I are gone. Her dad will never hear her call him daddy again and she will never again spend time with her friends-until heaven!

I will never again have the chance to say all the things I want to say to her-until heaven. I thought that I would watch her grow and develop into a beautiful middle-aged woman. I thought there was so much time left; now my little girl is gone and our family is hurt and broken. At the time I am writing this, she has been gone for six and a half months. I still feel at times the last few months have been a nightmare and I will wake up soon.

I don't understand the why of her death. I still get angry (I'm sure God understands my anger). I ask God how he could have let such a wonderful Christian woman like my Jennifer die that day and in such a terrible way. I want Him to give me an audible answer, but I know my answer won't come until heaven. I also know that God understands my pain and the day will come when He will wipe away my tears. Until then I will trust in Him, and that He has everything under control. I believe that He was there the day she died and He helped her transcend into heaven. Thank you, Lord for walking with her that day, and that she was not alone.

I have often wondered since Jennifer's death what I would say to someone when they ask me how many children I have. Last week a woman patient at my work asked me that question. I hesitated a moment and said: *"I have a beautiful daughter in heaven and two sons here."* That opened quite a conversation; I learned about some of her pain, as she learned about some of mine. In the end we prayed for one another. I now have more compassion, especially for those who have lost children.

To my Jennifer-

I miss you so much. The pain is unbearable at times. I am so lonely for you and all the things we will never do here on earth. I have a hole in my heart big enough to drive a bus through. I walk through life with no joy or hope of having any; people tell me that will change over time. I'm not sure I believe them. My dear friend, Elizabeth says to hang on, life is short, and I will be with you soon. She tells me I am doing great and that I am an example to others (both Christians and non-believers) as they watch how I handle this. Some Christians might choose to walk away from God and never serve Him again, saying He didn't answer their prayers. That is a heavy burden at times. I know I must stay in control when I don't feel in control at all. I am thankful to God for walking with me. I will not walk away, my dear Jennifer. I will love and serve God for the rest of my days.

Jennifer I miss your smile, your laughter, your voice, your smell and your touch. I even miss you telling me what to do and not to do- even though it was somewhat annoying. I still pray that Jesus will bring you back from the dead like he did Lazarus or let you send me a message in a dream or a vision. I pray each day that the Lord will see me through. My strength comes from Him. Only He will take away the torment in my mind and give me peace and joy.

Jennifer, I long to be with you in heaven: I long to see your beautiful smile again and to hear you sing about the Lord. Until then I will do the best I can here on earth, I will persevere, I will try to be more like you. I am proud to call you my daughter.

As the song goes by Steven Curtis Chapman: *"SEE heaven is just what He said it was and so much more,"* I look forward to that day when I meet you in heaven. You will take me by the hand and say: *"Hi, Mom. I have missed you, let me show you around."* What a glorious day that will be!

Miss you and love you forever,
Mom

Special Foreword by
Ken Paulson

Jennifer Ann Paulson is my daughter. She was my first born; my only little girl. She was a daughter every father would dream of and love to have. I feel so privileged to be her father and she is totally irreplaceable in my heart. No matter how much I wanted to always protect and keep her safe, the Lord Jesus Christ is the one who was in control of Jennifer's life. Jennifer lived her life for Him, and on February 26, 2010, she died wrapped in His loving arms.

There are people that go through life seemingly unnoticed. They don't clamor for attention by parading their accomplishments before others. They live ordinary lives with compassion, discipline, and integrity. Jennifer was just such a person. However, her life was anything but ordinary.

Jennifer was passionate about everything in her life: family, friends, teaching, and the Lord Jesus. Because of this passion, she made sure she was able to spend quality time with friends and family. She never forgot a birthday or anniversary, and she was typically the initiator of "get-togethers." Her passion for education and teaching led her to earn a special education teaching degree from Seattle Pacific University. She graduated with 290 credits in five years. She then went on to receive her Master's Degree from the University of Washington Tacoma, and at the same time was pursuing her Professional Teaching Certificate. This was done while she was teaching full-time at Birney Elementary School. The day before her murder, she had sent in the final paperwork necessary for completing this program; and one month later I received her certificate in the mail. Her passion extended into the giving of her time and resources, not because it was the right thing to do or because it was part of her job. She recognized that her abilities and finances weren't meant only for her; she gave of these to others as well.

Every person was of value to Jennifer. When I think of Jenny, I don't remember her ever speaking unkindly of anyone. Even when she knew of someone who had problems, she always spoke of them in a way that was filled with hope of the possibility of change and then she backed up this belief with constant prayer for that individual. Some of her students spoke of her classroom being a safe place for them and that they could tell her their secrets. She will be remembered as a kind and merciful person by many.

Jennifer knew she could help children reach higher. Teaching was not drudgery to her, she thrived doing this. A former school official said to me after Jennifer's memorial that "we need more Jennifer's." I hope that Jennifer's life will be an example and challenge others in their teaching career.

Words cannot begin to describe Jennifer's life and the impact she had in such a short amount of time. People often tell me that the first thing they remember about Jenny is her bright smile and sparkling eyes. Now her smile is missed by her students, co-workers, friends and family.

My wife, Cindy, and I were talking and decided more personal thoughts needed to be said, but I just wasn't able to. The next three paragraphs are her words.

Jenny would call Ken about everything. She not only valued and desired his input into her life and the decisions she was making for her life, but she loved her father dearly and wanted a real and close relationship with him. So we could expect calls most evenings around 8pm; the time just after she arrived home and ate her dinner. They would talk about what Ken thought about current events both locally and national, how her car was or wasn't running and what he thought should be done, or any issues she had with her house. She would ask if he had heard recently from Mark or Jason (even if she had asked this the previous night) and if he had, he would be required to give blow by blow details of their conversations. I am sure she came away a little disappointed as Ken, not as verbal as Jennifer, would probably not have gone into as much detail as she would have liked to have heard. Sometimes she would just call, not to really discuss anything. I think she just wanted to hear her daddy's voice and know that she was dearly loved. Every phone call ended with, "Love you, Jen."

Saturday mornings when the phone would ring, we knew it was Jenny. I am sure she waited as long as she could to call – wanting to be considerate of the possibility of us sleeping in. Saturday conversations typically included what our plans were for the weekend and what projects or adventures she had planned as well. The first few months after her death, we were acutely aware that the phone doesn't ring on Saturdays like they used to. And oh, how we miss that phone ringing.

When we would have a family get together, I could count on Mark, Jason and Ken harassing Jenny about the fact that she never had to buy her own car, as Ken always had bought the car. She would just smile and say that she was so thankful, even if the car was dented, spray-painted and not new and sophisticated like ones others may drive. From there the loving harassment would continue to how many cars she blew up – to use their terminology. There Jenny would step in to defend herself that most of the cars had something seriously wrong with them to begin with and therefore could not be classified as her fault. How we miss her loving presence in our lives.

When people die in the prime of their lives, they leave all those they loved behind. I never knew how many people Jennifer effected until her death. I continue to have numerous people call, write, or come up to me at the store or at church; to tell me the kind of person that she was, and that how she lived made a difference in their lives.

At her graveside service, her pastor since junior high school said that we had an investment in heaven that is more today than the day before. How true it is! On Friday, February 26th, 2010 at around 7:30 am, Jennifer was here with us, and the next heartbeat she was in eternity. She died to this world in a split second. Jennifer is now in heaven with her grandparents and other family members who preceded her in death.

Her death is such a dichotomy. With her death came sorrow, pain and joy. We have sorrow and much pain because we miss her tremendously, but at the same time we have joy for Jennifer because she is with the Lord and has received her reward.

Jennifer loved and pursued the Lord Jesus Christ with all her heart. If she were here today she would want you to know where you will spend eternity. My prayer is that Jennifer's life will give you the desire to seek what she has.....eternity with God the Father, God the Son, and God the Holy Spirit. If you want what Jennifer has, do what Jennifer did. Our lives are like a vapor that is only here for a moment when compared to eternity. May Jennifer's bright and shining life continue to shine and not be forgotten.

Love you, Jen!
Dad

Introduction by Author

The story of Jennifer Ann Paulson, at first thought, appears to be a story of unimaginable grief and painful sorrow. This is the story of a woman so young and full of selflessness and compassion, who was torn away from her family and a world that so desperately needed her. What took place early on that Friday morning in February was one of the most sadly horrifying events in Pierce County's public school history; an event that left in its wake a heavy burden of devastation, as family and friends seek tirelessly for answers as to why this happened – but that is not THIS story.

The newspapers, radio and nightly news has its own spin on this so-called tragedy. They will use words such as: murder, stalker, slain, harassment, shooting, and death to name a few. They tell their own story and seem to thrive on the grief of those involved and they consider Jennifer a victim- but that story is far from true.

On the contrary, the real story of Jennifer Ann Paulson is a story of hope, joy, compassion, forgiveness, purpose and celebration. She was born and raised to live her life for others. She understood at an early age God's calling on her life and never once took her eyes off the Master's bidding. She lived her life shining a light before all men, and walked this earth with strong convictions and dedication to her faith in Christ.

This is a story of how, even through tragedy, God heals, restores and uses every pain of human existence to show the hope of His salvation, and Jennifer's story is just that: hope. So forget all the words that the media will use to describe Jennifer, for you will not read them here. She was not a victim – she was a disciple. She is not dead – she is alive. Her life was not wasted – she fulfilled her calling.

Jennifer accomplished more in her thirty years on earth than many of us will accomplish in one lifetime. Each and every one of us has a God given destiny, a pre-determined course for our lives to follow. I wonder how many of us have discovered our true calling, thus preparing the kind of legacy we will leave behind. Jennifer sure did. She knew her course, followed her map, and trusted her Captain.

Even as I sit here now, penning the words of Jennifer's amazing life, I am a product of her ministry, a destination on the map God drew for her. During my most godless and rebellious days, she saw me as Jesus saw me.

She reached out a friendly hand to me and helped pull me up out of my sins. It has been to this day, one of the most divinely designed moments of my life. And I share it with you, in honor of Jennifer Ann Paulson.

Jennifer and I had grown up together since the very beginning. I am only a few months older than she, and since our families were close we became the best of friends. I will now admit publicly to playing Cinderella, Care Bears and My Little Pony- but it didn't matter, she was my friend. As time passed on I came to the astute realization that she was a girl, and they were not acceptable to play with. Fortunately, her younger brother Mark (who is still one of my dearest friends today), was just a few years younger than myself so he fit the bill perfectly. I remember many days and nights spent plotting and terrorizing young Jennifer - all because she just wasn't one of the boys.

Years passed on and I realized once again that she was a girl, and quite easy on the eyes. Despite my efforts to impress her, I felt my years of torment and pranks had caught up to me. But through all the years, she remained my cherished friend.

Adolescence snuck up on us both and we were faced with normal teenage decisions: Sex? Drugs? Rock and Roll? She chose wisely and followed hard after the Lord. I, on the other hand, chose a different path and fell into sin. Although we began to grow apart, she and I did keep in touch every so often. I even attended Life Christian Academy for a semester during a "break" from public schools and I remember, in detail, a few lectures from Jennifer Paulson. But not until years later, on Father's Day in 1999, did any of them ever take.

I remember it as if it was yesterday: the slightly gray, overcast sky, the restlessness in my heart; even the smell and sounds of the restaurant I was working in at the time. I was getting off of my Sunday shift and had almost reached my car in the parking lot when I realized I had forgotten my hat. I retraced my steps, and after a few minutes I had retrieved it and set off again. But as I approached again the doors to the restaurant, I bumped into Jennifer, who was out with her dad and brothers to celebrate Father's Day. I was very excited to see them and cancelled all my plans that afternoon; which included partying with my friends.

During the course of our meal and our fun-filled reunion, Jennifer invited me to a revival meeting at a local church the following Thursday. I wasn't too interested at first, but given our history and my respect for her lifestyle, I agreed.

Over the course the week that followed, Jennifer called me two times to remind me of the service. I assured her I had not forgotten, and as the day finally arrived I met her and a few of her friends at the church. I sat through the entire service a bit amazed at how freely she worshipped. She would raise her hands and praise God with no hesitation or shame, even with me sitting next to her. Jennifer was completely abandoned to the Lord.

The service's end finally came and they gave the usual altar call. I felt as if my heart were beating out of my chest – God was saying enough is enough. I immediately stepped to the front of the sanctuary and gave my heart back to the Lord.

During the weeks that followed I would go with Jennifer to those revival meetings and talk with her about how God was changing my life. After a while I got involved with a young men's group and didn't need Jennifer's accountability anymore. I am still involved with that church to this day.

Whenever anyone asks me my testimony, I always revisit that Father's Day in 1999. I recollect about how I forgot my hat and was reunited with my oldest friend who would be instrumental in me finding the Lord. I often wonder: What if I hadn't forgotten my hat that day? What if I had taken the back door? What if Jennifer had chosen another restaurant that day? All I can conclude is God had a plan for me and it involved her.

Now I am here to return her favor, and bring her story to you full circle to repay what she did for me. What she did was simply shine a light and lead me to Jesus. Through His work in my own life since that day, I have seen many people come to know the saving grace that found me. I have now been happily married for nine years to my wonderful wife Naomi (who also attended those revival meetings), and I have four beautiful children: Elijah, Cedar, Legacy and Harmony. I own my own home, I have a career, I am a contributing member to my community, church and family. All made possible because of Jennifer's commitment to sharing Christ with those around her.

I write this book to honor her legacy, to honor and support her family and to share the light she shined to all who read this book. Jennifer Ann Paulson modeled her life after the one who paid the ultimate sacrifice for all of us and the One who met a supposed tragic end just as Jennifer did – but in that end He rose again. And so did she. Although her family and friends will always grieve and miss her terribly, this will only last for a brief moment.

I have done my best to bring to you moments from every year of

Jennifer's life. Many memories and stories come from her dear friends and family; with a few of my own. I became inspired to live for God by writing this; and I hope you become inspired by reading it.

So despite what you have heard or read, this story is a story of triumph, celebration and healing. Now you will come to know the woman who touched so many and made a definite impact for the kingdom of heaven. Jennifer still lives on and through these pages you will live, love, laugh and cry just as she did.

For this is not the story of a tragedy, this is the story of a life well lived.

In loving memory of
Jennifer Ann Paulson
June 23, 1979
to
February 26, 2010

Always Cherished,
Always Loved,
Always Honored,
Never Forgotten.

"In the same way, let your light shine before men, that they may see your good works and praise your Father in heaven."

Matthew 5:16

Part 1: Faith

" And now these three remain: faith….."

From the Journal of Jennifer Ann Paulson:

1-4-10
Dear Lord,
I pray that I will treasure your words more than my daily bread. I do not live on bread alone but on every word that comes from your mouth (Matthew 4:4). Thank you for decreasing my desire to mindlessly consume food. I depend on you for __everything__.
> *Love,*
> *Your Beloved Daughter*

Jenny,

I've known you since I came to L.C.S. in the 6ᵗʰ grade. You were not only my friend in class and on the playground, but in church too. Youth group at a big Assemblies of God church was a big change for a quiet little Catholic girl and you helped me make that change. I needed a friend by my side and you were that friend. Thank you for always being the person I could count on to be there on Wednesday night or a week of summer camp. We had so much fun but what I realize now what was most important that I was there. I was learning more about the Lord than I ever thought I could. I was developing a personal relationship with God, something I had always thought was impossible, and I was there because I had the assurance that my friend Jenny would be there sitting next to me. Thank you for that.

I'm looking forward to the hours and hours we will sit and chat together in heaven. It always seemed that when we talked we never ran out of things to talk about. If it had been a couple of days, minutes or even weeks we picked up right where we left off and time always seemed to fly by. When we got older we would meet for coffee......well, coffee for me, and tea and water for you. We would sit and talk about school, students, colleagues, family and just about any and everything.

I am so glad you were able to meet and spend time with my son. I regret that you will not be able to spend more time with him. I was sad for a long time, regretting things on your behalf, listing in my head all of these "life experiences" I felt you had been cheated out of, and then I realized this was silly. What you have with the Lord is so much greater than any earthly experience or blessing. You with your ability to in an insanely short period of time come up with an A+ paper or complete some seemingly impossible task, you have done it once again: you raced ahead of us all to our heavenly home. I look forward to the day when we can all be together again, laughing and talking endlessly about everything. I think you may need more than one cup of tea and water; we will have a lot to chat about.

Love,
Colleen Wilson

Chapter One

A Life Introduced
Present Day

As the face of the morning sun poked her head over the white crest of the Cascade Mountains and the birds began to fill the air with their new song; the world awoke once again. Alarm clocks across the country began to waken all those who had drifted off into the carefree world of dreams and reminded them of the day ahead. Children scrambled frantically to gather their books and homework, attempting to have breakfast before heading out the door to school. Mothers and fathers groaned over traffic and stock market reports, fastening ties, ironing blouses and rushing out the door to make it to the office on time. February 26, 2010 began as any normal Friday morning would.

In a world where there is life and death, where people come and go without a thought, where there is triumph and defeat, poverty and riches, justice and travesty, two simple questions are asked at the foundation for validating all of human existence: Why are we here, and where is God?

In this world that was plainly created for peace and harmony, it seems we have steered far from that course. As the children of the rich dine at exquisite tables, the children of the poor are left to scramble for their scraps. Women have become object of lust and fantasy, thus loosing their righteous appeal. All that's left of actual masculinity has seemed to become stifled by the search for political correctness. In this world where life is so cheap, men and women, boys and girls have now sought out their lives looking for the answer to the question: why are we here?

The search for God has become so liberal and so commercial it seems He can be found in any book, in any heart and in any way we choose. This world has made us out to be gods, and encouraged us to look inside of ourselves for what a true god looks like, yet still we are empty. We have found religion and rules and codes to follow but none of this helps us understand: Where is God?

As we ponder these questions seeking their meaning, we come across the story of one life that has answered those two questions in their simplest form – and that life is Jennifer Ann Paulson.

BROWN EYED GIRL

Born in Lakewood, Washington on June 23, 1979, Jennifer entered this world with one driving force behind her: to love God and to love others. Raised in a Christian home, and a part of a prominent family in Pierce County, Jennifer was given a lifetime of opportunities to blossom. As she grew, so did her level of compassion. This compassion continued to grow so strongly, with the desire for to mankind live to their full potential, that it led her down a narrow road – toward that morning in February, where her life on this earth, would come to an end.

Jennifer was a brown haired, blue eyed girl; the definition of a pretty girl to say the least. Her eyes shown bright and there was always a little flash of excitement behind them. Her smile was wide and welcoming and the corners of her mouth wore a definite path from ear to ear. She had big, white teeth and wasn't afraid to show them off in the form of that big smile. That very same smile was quite contagious and she was always very generous with it. Not often would you find a frown on Jennifer's face. Her face just could not form one.

When Jennifer would laugh it was a lot more that just her throat, it was as if her soul was being tickled ever so lightly with a hundred soft feathers. Her shoulders would bounce just slightly enough to animate and emphasize her giggle. Her laugh was very sincere and would always ring in your ear long after you left her presence. They say laughter is the best medicine; that's probably why she was rarely ever sick.

There was a purity to Jennifer's countenance as well, almost a holy glow about her, as if her spirit was more beautiful than her face. Her heart was big and tender, filled to the brim with the love God has for people. It always overflowed and whether you were a believer or not, after a conversation with Jennifer you always walked away feeling a little more valuable than before.

HOME IS WHERE THE HEART IS

Jennifer owned a small house in the southern part of Tacoma, Washington; a cozy two bedroom, one bath she could call home. Once inside you felt a part of the family. The atmosphere inside the walls of her home were inviting and nurturing. On the walls and shelves were pictures of family and friends; those who made up Jennifer's world. Words of encouragement and faith were scattered over doorways and windows to remind her of God's faithfulness and purpose for her life.

Hanging in her kitchen was something that may not seem that unusual to anyone and it wasn't; it was just a calendar. But what was so extraordinary about her calendar was how the dates were filled in. Jennifer never missed a friend or family member's birthday, anniversary or other special event. Marked out under the birthdays of her friends were listed their favorite candies. It may not seem like much to some, but this really showed Jennifer's heart for those she cared about the most.

Jennifer's office is where she spent many a sleepless night studying and preparing for the next day of teaching. She was always bettering herself with her studies. Not only was she a teacher, she was also a student. Lining her office shelf were many tutoring and counseling books, to help her better serve the students she took under her wing. Her desire was to better herself, in order to better others. She was a woman on a mission.

Jennifer also believed in fun and games; she couldn't always have her nose stuffed inside a book. She was an average girl: she loved America and apple pie to coin the phrase. Since she was single and had no children of her own much of her free time was spent with close friends and relatives. She loved dining out at different restaurants, trying new and adventurous foods. She loved going out to see the latest movie and shopping the many fine stores in Tacoma's Proctor district. She not only enjoyed spending time laughing with friends, but also deep conversations about life, love and the Lord.

THE TEACHER INSIDE

The mission that had filled Jennifer's heart since a young age was what drove her to become a teacher and a mentor. She believed in the convictions of that mission so strongly she furthered her education immediately following high school. She needed no time off for self-discovery or soul-searching; she had already discovered herself in Christ. She continued her education throughout her entire twenties, earning her Master's Degree a few weeks prior to her thirtieth birthday. She did not go to school or teach for herself – she did it for her students; to be a better resource for them, and to enable them to better themselves.

Jennifer was a special education teacher. She worked with those students who just needed a little extra attention during their education process. She was drawn to those who needed a helping hand. Others may look at them as underprivileged or slow, but Jennifer saw them the way they really were: pure gold and full of potential. She strived night and day to encourage them to find the worth inside themselves.

Kindergarten through fifth grade students was the primary ages that Jennifer instructed. She worked and teamed closely with other general education teachers to help her students get ahead in the classroom. She had special time with each of her students everyday in order to answer any questions or just to simply guide them through their learning process. She has been known to be stern at times but not out of frustration, only out of a caring heart. She would spend many hours after school working with other teachers and staff on dealing with some of the personal struggles some of her students had. She was also the first on board for any parent night or activity. Much of her work was teaming with the parents and encouraging them to stay involved. Jennifer was also a great listener and very open to any and all questions regarding her methods of teaching, or her work in general. It had to have been exhausting and trying at times, but her face never showed it, she just continued to smile. After all, her students were worth it.

Jennifer's students were her heart and soul. As a momma hen watches over, nurtures and feeds her baby chicks, Jennifer watched over her students – and they absolutely adored her for it. They would come to her in trust with their most private dreams, hopes, fears and anxieties, and she would always listen. She would never judge them or look down on them because of their private thoughts. She always lent a listening ear, and a tender heart; never exposing them, only building them up.

Jennifer's classroom was like a fortress with walls high and strong to protect the young people from the storms and attacks of life. As if no force of harm could befall them when they were in the safe presence of their beloved teacher. She taught them the basics, of course: Reading, writing and arithmetic. But beyond all that she taught them to love, to trust and to believe in themselves. Jennifer understood there is no grander achievement than that of the human spirit. Her heart longed to see her students overcome whatever obstacles they faced in their lives.

TOO GOOD TO BE TRUE

Contentment seems to be such a far-fetched concept. To be completely satisfied with the life we have been given is quite an undertaking these days. The world will tell us that we need money, cars, big houses filled with toys, designer clothes and relationships to fulfill us. But in these things actual contentment is no where to be found. It can and will only be found in the mission God pre-designed for us. Needless to say, Jennifer was content. She could have used her wealth of knowledge and education to do anything regarding profession, or could have chosen a career with a higher salary, thus receiving all the world had to offer. Fortunately, she knew better. She had no other desire than to be in the center of God's will for her life.

Jennifer almost seems too good to be true. A heart so pure, looks so fair, and an understanding of true purpose in her life seems like a fairy tale, but don't be fooled, she was not without her imperfections. Some may say she was a bit nit-picky; others might say she was borderline temperamental. Either way, she definitely had her pet peeves. For instance she had real difficulty with "bad lighting" in a room. If she was out to eat it was vital to the success and mood of the meal that the lighting be just right; at least according to Jennifer's standards. If the lighting was too bright or if there was too much talking in the restaurant, our dear Jennifer could get rather grumpy.

The comfort of Jennifer's car riding experience would also be of the utmost importance for the atmosphere of the journey. Even the temperature of the car needed to be just right. Not to much air circulating, but also no stagnant air could be tolerated either. The radio also had to be on her favorite station and at the right volume. Friends would just give her the controls much of the time just to keep the peace. As hard as it might be to believe that our selfless heroine could make a fuss or throw a fit about something as small as radio volume or lighting in a restaurant, we must remember: she was human, after all.

If you didn't know Jennifer well or had not spent much time with her, she *could* come across a bit ditsy. Not because she lacked intelligence, but because there was a light, easy going component to her personality; also because her eyelids might sag slightly as if she was deep in thought or falling asleep. It did clash with her temperamental side, but it was not an air-head quality. It was a satisfaction of life quality.

Jennifer might also be considered, by some, to be a borderline hypochondriac. She wasn't terrified of germs, to be sure, but she did have a fetish with the sun and her rays. Not an overboard fetish, but a sober realization that too much sun could lead to skin problems. She was constantly reminding friends and family to wear the proper sun block on hotter days. Also the smell of exhaust fumes from a car worried her a bit. If she was stuck in traffic, the windows had to be rolled all the way up, even if it was a hot summer day. She was also a healthy eater. Not wanting to take a chance with her health she was very careful about soda, alcohol and fast food. But make no mistake; eyewitnesses have confirmed stashes of chocolate and candy in various places at her home and work.

FAMILY MATTERS

Family was a monumental part of who Jennifer Paulson was. As the oldest of three siblings, she set quite a high standard of living and big footsteps for her younger brothers to follow. In a world where the family unit has been perverted and torn apart by gossip, slander, hatred and bitterness, Jennifer remained a solid pillar in hers. She was like a beacon on a hill for her brothers, cousins, nieces and nephews. Phone calls, birthday cards and visits, however simple, can keep a family close. Jennifer poured her life into her family to make sure that they stayed that way.

Mark Paulson is her oldest brother and the two of them are separated in age by twenty-five months. He grew up in his sisters footsteps, graduating from college with a degree in Biblical Literature. Jennifer was a valuable resource to him, helping with term papers and all night study sessions. Mark played the role of consulting younger brother, checking in on his sister to make sure her car was up and running and her sewer line was working properly.

The two of them grew up like any other siblings would: they played together, fought together and caused their share of mischief in their younger years. Many of these tales you will read about in later chapters, but through it all, Jennifer and Mark bridged the gap between brother and sister and became the closest friends.

Jason Paulson is the baby of the family and Jennifer's cherished little brother. He also had a hand in the mischief and sibling rivalry. Throughout childhood she encouraged and tutored Jason through his struggles with school. The value she saw in Jason's life helped shape him into the man he is today. He has just recently graduated from college with a degree in engineering and is embarking on a successful career, that all started with his big sister's help.

Saying that Jennifer was a daddy's girl would be a definite understatement. She absolutely adored her father, Ken, and spoke of him with the highest respect and adoration. His opinion and support was vital to the woman she became. He encouraged her to be independent and pursue God's calling on her life. He watched with tears in his eyes as she met success after success. As she grew up before his very eyes, he couldn't help but beam with pride at the woman she was, and is, and continues to be.

The relationship between mother and daughter is a unique, pure and loving one, and Jennifer's relationship with her own mother was no different. Nancy is the proudest mother on the face of the earth. She had nurtured and cared for Jennifer since the day she was born, and watched her grow up before her very eyes. The two of them have spent much time in laughter, tears and even a few disagreements over the years, but that is what built the relationship and made it strong. Nancy watched in awe as Jennifer blossomed from a little carefree girl in pigtails, into a beautiful and elegant woman. She was proud to no end as she watched her baby girl fulfill all that God had intended for her precious daughter.

A good and faithful friend in this world is hard to come by, but Jennifer was just that friend to so many. She was considered a constant beacon of hope, a reminder of God's grace to those closest to her. To her dearest friends Joellen McBee, Jessica White and Colleen Wilson (You will hear from their hearts later as well), she was considered a sister. They have been friends through the thick-and-thin of life and walked on the road of adolescence and womanhood hand in hand. Despite the opposition life may have thrown in their paths, Jennifer put the interests of her friends in front of her own. She was a selfless lighthouse, stationed on the shores of salvation, guiding her friends through life's troubled waters.

To sum it all up and explain Jennifer Ann Paulson in one phrase, it would be this: She loved the Lord and others fiercely. She had her imperfections, as do all of us, but she understood the simple fact that she was given one life, just one opportunity to make a difference and impact humanity and she did just that. And on the morning of February 26, 2010, we all began to realize just how big that impact was.

Chapter Two

A Family History

The heart of a woman may seem at times as complex and vast as a maze of dreams and ambitions that reach throughout eternity. They could be dreams of family, career, travel, adventure or things as simple as cooking exquisite recipes of world famous chefs, having coffee in exotic foreign locations or seeing the sunset on the longest day of the year over the peaks of the mountains. A woman may spend her entire lifetime striving towards dreams and ambitions that were conceived in childhood that she never shared with another human being. These dreams are what drive her and keep her moving forward on the difficult terrain of life's winding road. Jennifer Ann Paulson was, of course, no different.

Jennifer kept a journal throughout most of her adult life; a documentation of many of her successes, hardships, thoughts and memories. She expressed one of her secret dreams in her journal, the lifelong desire she had to, one day, own a house on the beach. Maybe she dreamed of a house with a view of the majesty of the ocean. It would be a house where the sound of the breaking waves of the tide would soothe the souls of the many friends and family she would invite to visit. It would be a house of healing and shelter from the everyday pressures of the world. Perhaps she would take off her shoes and walk down to the water leaving footprints in the sand behind her. She possibly would roll up her pant legs and wade out into the shallow of the water and she would lift her face up to the sun as the morning wind blew her brown hair across her face as she felt the peace of God's creation.

Dreams like this – however private and at times far-fetched – have to start somewhere. The fruit that produced the seed of this ambition had to fall from a certain tree. Even though the ambition for a house on the beach was most likely deposited in Jennifer's heart from conception, whether she knew it or not, she spent her life chasing that house on the beach; maybe not the actual house, but leaving those footprints for her loved ones to follow. In Jennifer's case, this particular dream began with her grandparents: Cliff and Selma Paulson. They had a house on the beach which was sold before Jennifer was born. However, her aunt and uncle also owned a beach house where many wonderful family memories for Jennifer were created – that must be where her dream began.

GRANDPA MEETS GRANDMA

Cliff and Selma met in the small, yet growing town of University Place in the shadow of the big city of Tacoma in Washington State. It was as if their meeting was of a divine design to create Jennifer's life. As destiny would have it, Selma grew up in the home behind Cliff's relatives.

Cliff Paulson, as most young men do, had an eye for all things beautiful. His keen eye took notice of the young Selma and his after-hour visits to his relative's house became more and more frequent. Selma's family lived near Cliff's cousins on the same little road in that then small, unincorporated corner of Tacoma called University Place. Time passed all too quickly and after Cliff proposed to the object of his affection, the two of them set out on a life's journey that would lead to the life of our very own: Jennifer Ann Paulson.

Our family tree and lineage is most important in understanding who we are today. The decisions and life choices our parents, grandparents and ancestors make will effect, even if only in a minor way, the path our lives will take. The mold of the Paulson family name started even before Cliff, and that was with his father.

THE FAMILY BUSINESS IS BORN

Cliff's father embarked on the trade of buying and selling with his brother in the first decade's of the twentieth century when the world became amazed by the first motorcycle; a motorized bicycle that ran on gasoline instead of man power. The design was simple, the motor small and basic, but the result revolutionized and gave birth to the motor sport recreation industry. Along with motorcycles he also began buying and selling jewelry. His father and uncle began to learn the business and scratch out a living that would unfortunately come to a partial halt as World War I came.

As time passed, so finally did war, the Paulson's were still on his road to business establishment. Cliff's father continued with his jewelry business and his uncle began trading in the automobile business and struck up a thirty year association with the Chrysler. His uncle's dealership was in downtown Puyallup, off of Meridian Street, where he traded from for years, and retiring in the 80's. The building and dealership are long since gone, and the newer Puyallup library and park is now on/near its place across from the city municipal building, but the heritage of the Paulson's still remains.

Time, as it always does, continued to march on, and Cliff and Selma were married. Cliff made a move to buy the Paulson store from his father. The store stood on 11th and K Street in the downtown Hilltop area of Tacoma. The business started with the selling of radios and small appliances. Eventually refrigerators, range ovens, televisions, washers and dryers and motorcycles were also for sale inside the walls of this family business. Cliff did his best to stay contemporary with what was coming out on the market.

COUNT 'EM: FIVE!

As business was booming and the Paulson family began to grow, Cliff and Selma had a house built in Tacoma, near the Narrows Bridge, on Fairview Drive; a two-story home large enough to raise five (count 'em: five!) growing boys. It had a nice view of the Puget Sound and was built complete with a swimming pool and diving board. A tall, green Laurel hedge created privacy around the perimeter of this backyard family gathering place. This house still stands today. This is the house where Jennifer's father Ken was raised.

Ken was the youngest of the five Paulson brothers: Gerald, Melvin, Bob and Steve. Cliff and Selma, as any other parents raising boys, had their hands full and mischief was not a stranger to the Paulson doorstep. Ken attended High School at Tacoma Baptist School in the southern part of Tacoma, while his brothers attended Stadium High School. Ken then went on to receive a degree from Pacific Lutheran University in Business Administration.

KEN'S CHOICE

Every day our lives we make decisions. Some of these decisions may seem minuscule; others may seem to shape the course of our lives. At the end of our lives, I believe we will look back upon the choices we made and will be surprised at how the littlest ones made the biggest difference. In the mid 1960's Ken Paulson ultimately made a decision that would shape the course of the generations that would follow him. By making this choice, he set into motion the chain of events that would shape and mold his beloved daughter and guide her down life's road, making her into the teacher and mentor she would ultimately become. As we all know the choices Jennifer made would impact lives.

In the Stadium District of Old Town Tacoma, there is an old, turn-of-the- century brick church that sits just a half block from Stadium High School. Now the building looks a bit worn now, despite all the restorations over the years. A black coated iron fence surrounds the building, but its clock tower stands high and its timeless architecture is still on display for all who pass by. This building has been, and still is, one of the most prominent church buildings in all of Tacoma.

This building is where that vital decision was made. Ken can still picture it to this day: a small room of the side of the children's chapel; other children touched by the same message that touched him and led him to accept the forgiveness of Jesus into his heart and life. That day in the back of that brick church building marked the day of that most important decision of Ken Paulson's life; ultimately not only for himself, but for his children as well.

Ken continued his relationship the Lord. When he was just in grade school, his folks moved the family to attend Life Center Assemblies of God in the heart of Tacoma. His mother had attended this church when she was very young, and can even be seen in some of the mid-century photographs from the campus on 12th and G Street in downtown. Life Center was, and has long been, the beacon of hope for all of Western Washington.

Cliff and Selma Paulson set the example for their boys in their involvement in the ministries of Life Center. Cliff joined, and remained, on the church board for many years, and was a constant pillar of support and advisor in many ministries and outreaches.

SO THAT'S WHERE SHE GOT IT

Cliff was also an example of Christ outside of the church walls. When Trinity Broadcasting Network made plans to set up a station in the Federal Way area, Cliff and Selma were some of the primary supporters and investors in order to get the ministry off of the ground.

Cliff was also a strong advocate in the Youth For Christ outreach. He and his wife strove to help younger generations reach their full potential in this life, both physically and spiritually. This same passion was passed down to their granddaughter Jennifer, who was also an advocate for youth in need.

So this is where our story begins, with those who followed Christ and walked in His ways before Jennifer was even born. Our ancestors are the ones who set the stage and pass on blessings (and sometimes curses) down through the family lineage. It is our job, as it was Jennifer's, to take the reins and continue on the path. We must be sure to step carefully, lest we forget: the foundation our lives lay will be passed on to those who follow us.

Unfortunately, as we all know, death is a part of this life and a natural step in the frail life cycle. In the late 1990's Cliff Paulson: the man, husband, father, grandfather, uncle, brother, son and friend went to be with the Lord. He lived his life to the fullest; he stepped carefully leaving footprints in the sand for those who followed. He raised five sons, was a loving husband and saw many grandchildren born and raised in his likeness – the likeness of Christ. He helped found a family owned business that is still in operation. As the sadness of his passing settled on the hearts of his loved ones, they were ever reminded of Who he lived his life for, and in that they found hope.

In her later years, Selma suffered from Alzheimer's disease. Although her body may have been frail and worn, her spirit was not. She lived at Life Center's assisted living facilities until a year before her passing. Then the Lord called her home. She served the Lord until her very last breath. Losing her grandparents was painful for Jennifer, but she followed the example the set for her and stayed strong in her faith; keeping those memories of Grandpa and Grandma in a special part of her heart.

The influence of Cliff and Selma was strong in the life of Jennifer Paulson. She longed to live life as they lived it. Not necessarily from the physical standpoint, but from the spiritual and emotional. The long lasting marriage, a life with roots deep in faith, hope and love, and ties with a family they cherished so dearly. That is why she longed for a house on the beach, not for the view or for the value of waterfront property, but for the people, those dear souls who would fill it with laughter and joy. Well, now she has her house on the beach, built on the shores of eternity. One by one all of us who make Jesus our savior will stop by for a visit, and fill her house with the laughter and joy she has always longed for.

Chapter Three

A Life Begins

Her first five years

Albert Einstein was quoted as saying *"Imagination is more important than knowledge"*. I have pondered this quote for many years and have finally come to realize its meaning: The ability to dream, to create, to push yourself as far as you can go and then some; that is more important than the facts already discovered. As a young child, the ability to imagine is one of the strongest components of a developing mind. For a child can create and see what may not actually exist, but what could come into existence.

One of my first memories with our dear Jennifer was on a summer afternoon when the two of us were about five years old. I have a picture of the two of us on that day, sitting on the platform of the Big Toy my dad built in the backyard of the house I grew up in; eating our lunch from Wendy's, surrounded by a few stuffed animals and blankets. I have that messy face that all little boys do and Jennifer has her chubby, round cheeks outlining that smile. I remember this day vividly, because it was the day that both Jennifer and I experienced the power of imagination.

Jennifer's plan after lunch was to build a Cinderella castle and line it with flower boxes, use the blankets as royal robes and have the stuffed animals be our royal advisors. What actually took place in our minds is near impossible to describe in words and limited to the memories of my youth. We were transported to a vast and ancient castle with marble pillars and high stone walls; surrounded by a moat complete with sea serpent.

Jennifer and I were king and queen of our kingdom, and we ruled justly. The kingdom spread before us like a beautiful tapestry; a peaceful village that we could proudly look down upon (we were actually looking down at the overgrown lawn) and the subjects adored us. How long we actually stayed in this fantasy world I don't remember (and I'm sure our mothers disrupted us at some point) but where we were, was someplace special.

The two of us would try again and again to get back to that place of amazing imagination, but to no avail. We would get the same stuffed animals, the same blankets, and even play the same childhood games but nothing worked. The point where our minds fired on the same link that day could not be duplicated. The innocence of a child and the mind of a child are the only things that could ever take someone to such a place. That's why it has always stood out in my memory: A special time with a special friend.

JENNIFER MEET WORLD

Jennifer Ann Paulson was born on June 23, 1979 and was greeted by the sun. It was early afternoon. Ken and Nancy were both exhausted from a long night of labor. She was born during an emergency c-section and Jennifer was introduced to the world; she had arrived and breathed her first breath of life. Nancy had quite a surprise when she was handed a baby girl, since she was convinced her baby was a boy. Flowers and dolls were brought to the hospital by excited friends and family, who just couldn't wait to see Jennifer's beautiful face.

Both Ken and Nancy fell immediately in love with her, as all parents do as they see their offspring. The midnight feedings, dirty diapers and sleepless nights were all part of raising this priceless vessel for God. Jennifer was the first child for both her parents but just another member of the ever growing Paulson clan of cousins. The task of raising this little princess wasn't taken lightly and she was dedicated to the Lord at Life Center by Pastor Fulton Buntain. A baby dedication is not like a Catholic baptism, it is just a prayer of trust that God will use that child for His purposes. We all know God used her mightily.

WALK LIKE A MONKEY

Jennifer began to grow leaps and bounds as all children do right before our very eyes. She was a normal first born child even before her brothers were born, being fussy about certain foods and quite set on having her way. She had those toddler cheeks that were a grandma's delight and a head of peach fuzz at first that caused her ears to appear bigger than they actually were. Those blue eyes of hers began to take on a light behind them, a spark of worth and value installed in her from those around her.

Jennifer began to crawl and cross the bridge from infancy to toddlerhood. Her crawling was most memorable because she didn't like her knees touching the floor. She would scoot around with her rear end up in the air with her hands and feet on the floor and shuffled along to get from one place to the next. Apparently, she almost resembled a monkey crawling in this way. It probably didn't do much for speed but it did save unnecessary wear and tear on the knees. Good thinking, Jennifer!

THE LITTLE ESCAPE ARTIST

The stories from our own childhood, the ones our developed mind has erased, are the ones we love to hear about the most. We can't help but grin and laugh at the memories of our earliest days usually told by a parent or close relative. Most all of us have heard over and over again the story from our parents of how we were lost in the supermarket or seemingly disappeared at the park, only to be quite close by; Jennifer was no different.

Jennifer grew up in a three bedroom, two bath, tri-level home on a dead end street named John Dower Road. It had a nice backyard with a big rock retaining wall and plenty of trees to play in and around. Once inside the front door a hallway led straight to the kitchen, off to the left was the lavishly furnished living room where no children were allowed (we of course entered many times). To the right were the stairs that led upstairs and a small set of stairs down to the family room. With all of these options any young child would have a great time exploring. But it was not what was inside the walls of security and familiarity that piqued Jennifer's curiosity: it was what was outside the walls.

Jennifer had a bit of hair on her head by then. Her face was that of any small child marked with innocent wonder of the world around her. Her walk was not so much a stride, but more of a wobble from one foot to the next. She began her day as any other: made a mess of her breakfast, had her morning diaper change, maybe even took a nap when she got grumpy. All the while she was waiting, waiting for that opportune moment to make a break for it – right out the front door. Before I go any further, all you parents out there take a deep breath. Okay, now I will continue.

John Dower Road (actually named for my great-grandfather), was purely residential, but the beginning connected to a busier cross street that ran in front of an elementary school not sixty yards from the Paulson home. Apparently young Jennifer made her way down the street and had almost arrived at the school before she was found by her frantic parents. She had only been gone for a minute or two, but to a concerned parent, those minutes can seem a lifetime.

These are the stories our parents jokingly hold over our heads in our adult life. We have absolutely no memory of them, and it is quite refreshing to hear these tales. Jennifer made it through her "great escape" unscathed and was none-the-wiser for what she had done. One thing is for sure though: God was watching over her that day. He had a plan for that little escape artist, and He was going to watch over her.

BITTER-SWEET BROTHER

In July of 1981, Jennifer got the bitter-sweet surprise of her life: she was no longer alone. There was another child crying in the night, receiving midnight feedings and vying for the attention of her parents. Mark Paulson was small when he was born; pictures would show his head to be the size of a softball. Now sibling rivalry could begin! She would now have to share her toys, her play space and her mommy and daddy. But they got along quite well – she needed someone to boss around.

Both Jennifer and Mark grew up in a family of jet-skiing, motocross racing and "anything else motor" sports lovers. At the tender age of three or four, some of the older Paulson cousins would strap a helmet over Jennifer's pigtails, slide on some gloves and let her at it. Mark, being all boy, took naturally to these extreme motor sports, but it may surprise you how fearless Jennifer was. She had just as much fun as the boys and wasn't afraid to "get air" over a jump on the dirt motorbike track. Now Nancy may not know, or has purposefully blocked from her memory, Jennifer's extreme motor sport escapades, so let's keep them between us. But this shows us Jennifer's fearless nature. Although she was concerned with certain health risks, she was not afraid to have an adventure.

In the early 1980's there was a Christian television program for kids called "Super Book". It was a serial cartoon that followed the adventures of two children, a boy and a girl, and their robot friend. During the opening credits the three would open up a Bible and whatever passage they opened it to, they would be transported to that place. This was one of Jennifer's favorite shows and a good and fun way for her to learn the stories of the Bible. She saw David fight Goliath, watched Noah build his ark, and walked with Jesus Christ Himself. Cliff and Selma would record this show along with "Flying House", another biblical adventure cartoon, onto VHS tapes for the grandkids to watch.

SPIRITUAL ROOTS

Life Center Assemblies of God Church had been a big part of Jennifer's life since the day she had been born. The tall arched ceiling of the foyer with its winding staircases leading to the upper level balconies, nursery and bride's room was a most familiar sight to her; this place was like home. As a child she would run and play in the long, maze-like hallways of her family's home church.

Gray Chapel, named for a prominent church member, with its stained glass picture of Jesus praying in the garden of Gethsemane while His disciples slept, was a big part of Jennifer's place of worship. She went to youth church, school chapel and later watched her father get remarried in the Gray Chapel. Years later, at the end of Jennifer's earthly life, her friends and family gathered to pray and comfort each other before Jennifer's memorial celebration. All this, all her spiritual roots, were at Life Center.

DADDY AND DAUGHTER DAY

Jennifer, like most babies, spent the church service time in the nursery. At the top of the winding staircase from the foyer, parents would drop off their precious babies into the care of the churches most trusted workers. The nursery ministry is the most important and vital ministry to a growing and family oriented church. No child is ever turned away, but Jennifer did almost overstay her welcome on one occasion.

It was a Sunday morning and Nancy was sick at home with the flu. No problem, Ken just strapped Jennifer into her car seat and off to church they went. It was father-daughter night. After arriving at church, Ken carried Jennifer up those winding, wide steps to the nursery: daddy and his little girl. Ken checked her into the nursery, made sure to kiss her goodbye and went down to the service. It was a great service as usual, and after it was dismissed Ken walked out into the foyer for a moment to visit with some friends, have a few laughs and then struck out for home. He got into his car, started up the engine and pulled out onto the road. But wait! Where was Jennifer? Ken immediately realized his mistake and hurried back to the church (he had not gone far) and retrieved his young daughter from the nursery. Jennifer was of course none the wiser and they set out again for home, this time together.

THE PACT

The great and most important thing about being a part of the family of God is the fact that every one of us has a place in it. Despite all the labels that the world may put upon us: worthless, failure, minority or outcast, God sees us in a different light. He has placed a gift inside each and every one of our hearts just waiting to be brought to fruition. These gifts can be unveiled even at the youngest of ages. Jennifer discovered even as a small child she had the ability to persuade others to her way of thinking. Now do not be mistaken, this was not a manipulation tactic, it was pure in every way – the teacher and evangelist inside of her being born; helping the people around her understand how she thought, and why they should think that way as well. Since she had the mind of Christ and a heart that was pure, the persuasion came easy. She was a teacher and mentor from the very beginning. That was a gift God placed inside her, a gift that required determination and boldness. Maybe this is why, as children, Jennifer and I would spend our play time imagining of Cinderella and Sleeping Beauty instead of GI Joe and the Ninja Turtles; because I saw things her way. It seems silly now, a little boy playing with girls' toys, but that is how well she used her gifting.

Jennifer began her long and successful education at Life Christian Academy, home of the mighty Cavaliers, and a part of the ministry of Life Center. She would continue from kindergarten all the way through twelfth grade at this school becoming a stronger and stronger pillar at Life Christian Academy (L.C.A.) every year. At the time Jennifer was entering school, L.C.A. was only instructing through eight grade and, as a Kindergartener, was taught by Life Christian's most famous and beloved teachers: Mrs. Kohl (who also taught Jason Paulson years later). She embarked into a new world of letters numbers and colors. She learned to write her name, add and subtract, and maybe the fundamentals of nature such as wind, gravity and light. She took to learning naturally, and it was quite apparent her ever developing brain had room for much knowledge.

As Jennifer was learning words, their sounds and spelling, she also discovered something else about them: the power behind the spoken word. Jennifer made many friends in her first year of school, some would come and go, and others would walk with her throughout her entire life. There was a particular friendship that was sparked by a pact; a promise made between two innocent little girls. The impact of the promise those two made would be carried out into their adult life, and for both of them, their ministries on earth began.

Jesus said, "Let the little children come to me, for the kingdom of heaven belongs to such as them." The faith of a child is without scales over the eyes, without prejudice, and without doubt. In the eyes of a child, anything is possible. The world is wide open for them to discover, dream and achieve. Only as adults do we become doubtful, hard-hearted, and set in ways that may not be the Lord's. The pure faith of those two little kindergarten girls helped them to see the calling of God in their own lives and helped them to see it in each other.

Jennifer and her young classmate had discovered the desire in themselves to serve the Lord, but not only that, to serve as missionaries. A missionary, at first mention of the word, is a white couple living in grass huts in the jungle, teaching indigenous people about a Jesus who they might not even relate to. A missionary makes the sacrifice of their home and comforts to bring this gospel to those people in the foreign mission field and for that we are grateful. But being a missionary isn't about what country you minister to, but who you minister to. Jennifer's young friend grew up, was married and to this day she and her husband are missionaries in the Philippine Islands. She told Ken and Cindy Paulson this story at Jennifer's memorial celebration. Touched by this, he asked me to share the story; the power of God's calling on young Jennifer.

We all know how Jennifer fulfilled her calling, and walked closely on God's path. She grew up and became an inner-city youth worker, teacher, and most importantly, a beacon of the good news of Jesus. So she stayed committed to the pact she had made when she was only five years old at Life Christian Academy. Although it may seem like only the innocence of a child's imagination and coincidence of circumstance, God was with those girls when they were very young, and he shaped them into women of impact.

Chapter Four

A Life Grows
Years 6-10

The difference between boys and girls is apparent during the first few years of life, and becomes even more so as childhood blooms. There is an old rhyme that holds sway over that difference and even though it is a cute little saying, there is truth behind the words: "Boys are made of snips and snails and puppy dog tails. Girls are made of sugar and spice and everything nice." God made men and women, boys and girls, entirely different and those differences need to be celebrated.

In a boy's eyes it is perfectly acceptable to play outside in the rain and mud. They are not too worried about their new clothes getting dirty, or catching a cold. Little boys don't always see the logic behind going indoors to use the bathroom, when a patch of trees will do just fine. Playing the hero is a huge part of a boy's day; Jedi knights, policemen, or fierce warriors are just a few of the roles a boy will play. They will lose themselves in capturing bad guys, in a high speed chase or on a fierce battleground in a faraway land. These things are healthy for a boy, for when they become men they will be the leaders for their wives, warriors for their families and heroes to their children.

A little girl is entirely different in nature from a little boy. Made of sugar and spice, a young girl will bring sweetness and flavor to the world around them and everyone in it. This is their calling and responsibility, and it is to be taken seriously.

When a girl is young she dreams of being a princess or a ballet dancer and will wear big, frilly pink dresses as they act out their fantasy. They play house, setting up their dolls around the table, pretending those dolls are her family. A girl will cook the doll's lunch and dinner, or host a party. As a little girl dances, sings, and twirls (most times to an invisible audience) our hearts are melted and our eyes will tear up at the joy they bring. Little girls are born to have big dreams.

Jennifer Ann Paulson was a girl through and through: She had big dreams. She loved to be the belle of the ball, with her flowing dresses, many given to her by Grandma Paulson. Her imagination was healthy and in full swing. Being the headline of the show, or star of the parade was not an uncommon day dream for her. She also loved to color and paint as do most young girls. She loved animals, especially dolphins. She even had a large, framed picture of a pair of dolphins jumping from the ocean her parents bought her for Christmas one year. All the things we hope for in our little girls, Jennifer was. Her childhood was shaping the woman she would become, and the way she could relate to children in order to become an effective teacher.

THREE'S COMPANY

Jennifer was approaching her seventh birthday and was quite content with the world around her. She had one younger brother she could play with and boss around. Many family photos were taken of the two of them smiling and laughing as Jennifer enjoyed being the oldest sibling. Mark was, of course all boy, so playing My Little Pony and Care Bears with him was out of the question (I guess that's why I played with them instead). They enjoyed the typical sibling fun: snowmen and sledding, going to the zoo and the fascination of the animal kingdom. And as to be expected, sibling quarrels.

In March of 1986, she received quite a shock when another little baby boy came home with Mom and Dad. Jason Paulson was the newest addition to Jennifer's life, and the third and final child for the Paulson family. Three truly was company for the Paulson children as they embarked on the adventure of siblinghood. Jennifer commemorated this event in her journal along with a few photos. Ken brought in a picture of newborn baby Jason to Jennifer's class at school for show and tell. Jennifer was not too pleased with that picture because, apparently, Jason was born into this world without clothes. Jennifer stated in that journal that the photo was both embarrassing and gross; but the boy in the photo became her most cherished baby brother.

CENTER STAGE

Life was beginning to take shape for Jennifer; growing out of childhood into the beginning stages of becoming a young woman. As a small child, everything is decided for you: when to sleep, when to wake, what to eat and what to wear. Jennifer now began to grow out of that period in her life, and began to pursue interests of her own. She participated in a Life Christian Academy production of "Psalty's Christmas Calamity" in 1988. She was a part of the team of choreographers (I remember this production because I was also involved and had the worst chapped lips of my life during the entire show.). Our job was to dance and act out the words to the Christmas carols in boy and girl pairs with our only prop being a large box. This took a lot of rehearsals and extra trips to the school for Nancy to pick up and drop off young Jennifer, but it was worth it to let her daughter spread her wings.

A few years prior, Jennifer had decided to try her hand at a stringed instrument: the violin. She was only five or six years old at that time and supported by both her parents to take on the challenge. Certainly there must have been some trying practices around the Paulson household, and it must have been frustrating at times for a young girl to learn the violin. What it must have instilled in her, though, was discipline and a desire to meet her goals.

As time went on she became a better and better violinist and had the opportunity to perform in Life Center's annual Singing Christmas Tree. She performed a duet with another violin student a year younger than she. The Singing Christmas Tree has been a Life Center event for decades and a community kick-off for Christmas time. People from all around the city gather together to celebrate the true meaning of the season – and that is Jesus.

As a young girl, Jennifer must have been as excited as could be about performing and showing off her talents. What made this so special was that this was her first ministry at the church she would attend her entire life. She was developing a desire to minister to people with God's love.

CRUEL AND UNUSUAL PUNISHMENT

As children, Mark and I often embarked on hunting trips. Not for elk, moose or some other pristine animal, but for bees. We would capture them in glass jars, twist the lid on and put them in the freezer. Many of you men out there, I'm sure, did this as boys. It helps fill the void between playing with G.I. Joes and tossing the football. We would capture these fierce predators in glass jars, twist on the lid and, after removing useless things from the freezer such as beef, juice and chicken, place the bee-filled jars inside. We would wait excitedly for a few minutes as the insect began to freeze, thus leaving it in a comatose state. Then after removing the frozen jars, we would watch in wonderment as the bee would return to life. We would release it back into the wild and then repeat the entire process all over again.

Jennifer was not too keen on this pastime of ours and would lecture us endlessly. She would go on and on about importance of the environment, taking care of God's creation and other things little boys don't care about. She claimed it was cruel and unusual punishment. We never took her lectures to heart until one day she took a stand. We put our usual jars into the freezer, and as soon as our backs were turned she snuck into the kitchen and set the captives free. Then it was every man (and woman) for themselves. Her heart was in the right place, but she should have set them loose outside and not in the kitchen! I still remember her frantically yelling (hilarious, but frantic) as those bees swarmed after her.

Jennifer always had a tender heart for God's creatures. No matter how big or small Jennifer cared about them. Jennifer would even defy the will of two destructive young boys to look after God's creation.

THIS ONE'S FOR THE BEES

One of the most famous stories of Paulson family lore also involves bees. Their home in Lakewood had a small clump of pine trees in the backyard, and was thus a hunting ground for a hornet's nest. Boys, for some reason, have an internal urge to knock down these nests of doom, despite the risk. Why they will risk life and limb to satisfy this desire is anyone's guess, but we do know it is part of a little boy's DNA, and that summer day was no different.

Jennifer was inside her family room playing while Mark, a few others and I were outside playing with a Frisbee. We had noticed earlier that day a big hornets nest hanging in one of the trees. It was if Mother Nature had painted a target on the hive as we began pelting the hive with the Frisbee. Jennifer came out a few times during this process to remind us that we were morons and would surely get stung.

After a few minutes the hive tumbled down from that tree and we had victory; or so we thought. The hornets did not appreciate this and all the boys scattered and began screaming and running frantically for safety. Jennifer heard the yelling, realized the situation, and shut the back sliding glass door, locking it to insure no hornets would enter. This would have been a great idea had Mark not been making a dash for the same door. As

I'm sure you can imagine, much yelling ensued as Mark yelled at Jennifer and Jennifer yelled at Mark. Finally, the back door was opened and Mark found safety. I had entered through the front door without being stung and met up with the siblings in the family room. As Mark ripped off his clothes inside the sliding door, the room was filled with angry hornets, thus ensuing more chaos for Nancy, young Jason, and all other innocent bystanders.

The situation was finally resolved and the wounds were tended to. This story has been constantly recalled through the years at family gatherings and reunions. This one is definitely for the bees.

SHIRT OVERBOARD

Another fun Paulson family memory involves another confrontation between the two siblings. Cliff Paulson owned a restored sixty-three foot Air and Sea rescue boat from World War II. He had it refurbished in the fifties and could then entertain family and friends for a day of boating on the Puget Sound. The boat had a deck on the rear for fishing or lounging in the sun; there was a small kitchen and restroom in the hull and even had a small table for eating or playing games. The cabin on top was spacious enough to put passenger seats inside so eager boaters could get the Capitan's view of the open water.

One sunny Saturday the Paulson family was out for another fun day of boating. The sounds of excited children running around the boat filled the air. It would be a day to remember. Jennifer, Mark, Jason and a few friends and cousins were in the hull of the boat playing. Somehow Jennifer got her hands on Mark's shirt. She began tossing it around and twirling it over her head teasing her young brother. Unfortunately for Mark, one of the small, round, porthole windows was open and as Jennifer swung that shirt around, out went the shirt. Jennifer claims it was an accident, and has always stuck by the story; Mark has a different opinion of the matter. Either way, that shirt was never seen again.

There is a picture in the Paulson family photo album of that day. Family and friends gathered together on the hood of the boat, each person with a big smile and tired faces from a day of fun; every face except for Mark. He was wearing his mother's sweatshirt and his face had a big frown from the loss of his shirt. He was quite irritated with his sister that day. Now that day memory is one of his most cherished.

A-TEAM

Jennifer began to excel in the world of academics as she climbed the ladder of grade school. She was instructed by some of the many gifted teachers and her name would be found on the A-list honor roll at school month after month. She enjoyed learning the names, dates, and places of the World's history. She began to understand numbers and how they worked. But what she enjoyed most about school was those people around her. She reached out to the new student who needed a friend, and scooted her chair close to those children who struggled with the school work, so they could find the success she had been blessed with. God was molding her heart to be like His Son's.

COLORING CHAMPION

Jennifer also enjoyed being artistic, loving to color and paint. She entered a coloring contest at the local Red Robin family restaurant. The challenge was simple but the entry needed to be precise. A blank coloring sheet of the Red Robin was given to each child who entered and the task was to color the bird to the best of their abilities. Jennifer entered her colored picture and waited anxiously for the results. Well, lo and behold, Jennifer took first place in the contest and won a brand new bike for her efforts. She was quite proud of herself, and didn't mind bragging a bit while showing off her new bicycle to her friends. She was a coloring champion.

SNACK TIME

One of a child's favorite times of day is definitely snack time. Jennifer, believe it or not was not too much into sweets or candy (unless it was a strawberry milkshake) and definitely did not like graham crackers. She did, however, fall prey to a snack sensation that sweeps through a lot of young grade school children, and that snack is Play-Doh. This putty is used to make cut out animals and roll and flatten with a child's imagination. Children will spend hours shaping and forming different works or art and getting it all over their clothes and all over the carpet. This dough can be found in almost every school and church classroom across the country.

Jennifer enjoyed playing with Play-Doh, but as many children do, she found another use for it. She had it down to a precise science. She would roll up the dough into little malt ball-size spheres and enjoy a salty snack. Sharing was also very important to Jennifer and with two younger siblings she became quite good at it. She loved to share her Play-Doh snacks with the other children and encouraged them to partake with her in imagining any flavor that they wanted. Teachers and Sunday school volunteers always wondered where the Play-Doh went. Well, now they know.

THE HEART OF A CHILD

Jesus said we must become like little children, for the Kingdom of Heaven belongs to such as them. What did He mean? I believe He meant we must have a heart that is pure and innocent before Him. We must learn to rely on Him for our needs, and thank Him for all that we have. A young child has complete dependence on their parents, and needs them for everything that they do. As a child grows older, they become independent and don't need or want their parents help as much. We must keep our heart in constant wonder because all good things come from God.

The world we live in today is doing its best to steal and destroy the souls of young children. There is abuse, neglect and abandonment in every corner of the planet and the broken souls of children lay scattered. Whether a child lives in the poorest slums of India or in the home of America's richest business tycoon, the innocence of childhood is under attack. To protect the precious souls of children is a full time battle and many times turned down by those closest to them. Parents who are not ready for children or don't want a child at all, fathers who abandon their families at the first sign of responsibility, or a mother who feels inadequate to do the job. Either way what is left behind in the ashes is a little human being who will grow up with fear of abuse, self esteem issues, anger and resentment toward the world. But God! God has always saved a remnant of people to care for and minister to these broken souls, no matter the cost. He has hand selected a special group to reach out to them, and we all knew one of those people in Jennifer.

Jennifer began to feel the hand of Father God begin to shape and mold her heart even at the age of five and six years old. She began to have a heart for those Jesus had a heart for. She had special eyes for those who struggled in school or who didn't have the social skills to fit in with their peers. Her heart was tender to the souls of those the world had done its best to ruin. Well, I've got news for you dear reader: no one would be left behind, not on Jennifer's watch!

This is what set Jennifer Ann Paulson apart from those around her. When others would turn their backs, she would reach out her hand. Not because she was better or because God loved her more, but because God's plan and design for Jennifer was so detailed and specific. The world needed Jennifer Paulson.

INTERLUDE

Jesus Christ was born into this world with one purpose in mind, one goal to accomplish: He came to seek and save that which was lost. Not only did He plan on saving them, but He sought them out. He got down on His knees in the dirt and looked into the eyes of people that were broken and ruined. He did not spend much time with rich, successful, upper-class people who had no desire to change their hearts. On the contrary, He spent his time with fishermen, tax collectors, beggars and lepers. His heart was drawn to those who society deemed worthless. He became a friend and teacher to many; teaching, serving and listening.

In the end, the people whom Jesus loved and reached out to, mentored and believed in, betrayed Him and turned Him over to be executed. They nailed Him to a cross like a common criminal. He was humiliated and beaten, all the while begging God to forgive their sins. In the midst of His torture, His care was for the souls of the people. Jesus Christ died hanging on that cross, but even with His dying breath, He spoke words of life to one of the criminals hanging on the cross next to Him.

Those of us who have accepted the fact that Jesus hung on that cross for us and who can admit our personal need for a savior, are now His light in the world. We have accepted that salvation and Christ's Spirit now lives in our heart. We are called to be a light in dark places just like Jesus was, and shine it for those He died for. The only light that can rid the world of darkness is the light of Christ, and Jennifer Ann Paulson let that light shine her entire life.

After graduating high school, Jennifer was a student at Seattle Pacific University. In order to help support herself, (besides calling dad) she worked a part-time job in the University's cafeteria. She would bus tables, clean dishes and work on the food line. It was a humble job, but Jennifer was a humble girl and it fit perfectly with her class schedule. It helped her to break the grind of daily classes, term papers and homework. Since she was such a bright and friendly girl, she made friends instantly.

One of the dishwashers who lived in the area and who seemed to have a sadness about him. Jennifer, being the light that she was, befriended this young man. The relationship between the two of them was strictly plutonic and they would chat about the weather, life in general and God. What Jennifer discovered inside this young man was a God-ordained destiny wrapped in a blanket of hurt and insecurity. Jennifer constantly encouraged him to pursue the Lord and find his identity in Christ.

Jennifer continued to live like Jesus lived, allowing the Holy Spirit to use her to reach this young man. She would pray for him and encourage him to visit her church. As time went by, he left his job and Jennifer graduated. The two of them didn't speak for quite some time.

Now there is something that must be made clear: Jennifer never led this young man on. She never flirted with him or indicated any romantic interest. There were no meetings outside the school that would give him the wrong idea. She didn't do anything wrong or irresponsible. She simply was a light for others to see.

Part 2: Hope

"…..hope….."

From the Journal of Jennifer Ann Paulson:

6-3-08
Dear Lord,

I want to become a prayer warrior. I want to be a woman of prayer who experiences Your power in me and sees it working in others. I want to pray for Your will to occur. I want to see lives changed. What will be the catalyst for me to become more disciplined with prayer and fasting? I commit to it this summer. I need a breakthrough. I need Your guidance. I want my life to reflect the will You have for me.

Please help me to not be fearful of releasing control to You. You have an abundant life planned for me. Please help me be willing to step out and accept it. Please help me to humble myself and accept it. Please help me to trust You and accept it.

Jenny,

You are unique, funny, wacky, loving, kind, adventurous, patient, sweet, and in short the best friend I ever had or will ever have. I miss you every moment of every day. You were the best listener, the best encourager, and the best talker I have ever known. I think back to our last conversation a couple of days before you died, and I remember how you said that you loved me and thanked me for being your friend and for supporting you. I told you I loved you back and that I was, of course, always here for you. I remember thinking that we didn't say we loved each other enough, but I thank God everyday that we did that night. I thank Him every day for giving me the chance to experience true friendship, one that of course had its ups and downs, but which also let each of us be authentic and real with each other. As much pain and grief that I have struggled with over the past year, as much as my heart aches to pick up the phone and hear your exuberant voice say: "It's me!" I wouldn't change one moment of our friendship. It was the ride of a lifetime!

Jessica White

Chapter Five

A Life Enjoyed
Years 11-15

Mankind, since the beginning of creation, has strived and pushed to the limit of our potential. Humans have had the innate desire to defy Mother Nature, and to discover the vastness of this universe. The depths of the oceans, the caverns that lead deep into the earth, the active volcano, the highest mountain and the fiercest storm – all have fascinated us for centuries. Scientists find logic and reason behind these wonders, discrediting the Creator of the universe. They have broken down our own creation by claiming we evolved and that this amazing earth and galaxy was a cosmic accident; but believers in Jesus know better than to believe these claims.

Our God is a God of majesty, power and perfect holiness. The sight of a waterfall, blooming flower or beautiful sunset, show us God's peace and His beauty. A tornado, earthquake or hurricane, remind us of God's ultimate power. The birds of the tropical rainforest, the grizzly bear of the mountain and the mallard on a nearby lake, remind us God gave us this world to rule. We rule as governing creature, but we also rule with respect of God's creation.

As we look around at all that God created; at His handiwork, we find Him. All the attributes that make Him God can be found through out His creation. We come to realize that God may not be the God religion has made Him out to be. He is God alone and we must conform to Him and not the other way around.

A sense of adventure has been placed inside every one of us. Looking at all God has made for us to enjoy, we realize He is a God of adventure. Different people will respond to it in different ways and that is what makes the differences between humans so amazing. Jennifer had that adventurous spirit in her since the day she was born and responded to it in the only way she knew how: she went for it!

SEVEN SHADES OF DORK

The next story I will share with you is my personal favorite Jennifer Paulson memory. We were both approaching our teenage years and since she was born into a jet-skiing family, I reaped some of those benefits as well.

One of Jennifer's uncles has a house on the Puget Sound and would allow family and friends to stay on weekends and holidays for fun on the beach and in the water. I would trek along for weekend getaways with Jennifer, Mark, Jason and their parents to this amazing A-framed house. Mark, Jason and I would busy ourselves with important things, such as catching crabs and making them fight, throwing rocks at jellyfish and digging for clams we would never find. Jennifer no longer annoyed me as a little girl, but made me nervous now as an attractive young woman. I would spend my time with Mark and the boys, but had an eye on that young beauty and would find excuses to go play next to where she was. I was as discreet as possible so the boys wouldn't notice my interest. Unfortunately for me, Jennifer knew I was seven shades of dork and there was no impressing her.

On one such weekend excursion, Jennifer asked me to go for a ride with her on one of her dad's jet skis. I didn't really care to be taxied around by her, but the thought of being close to that blooming beauty overturned the reasoning about a boring "girl ride". Unfortunately it backfired, because I forgot who I was dealing with. Jennifer was a fabulous jet skier and I should have known the ride would be anything but boring.

Jennifer's dad checked out our yellow life jackets with blue safety straps (I wouldn't be surprised if Ken still has them) and after a lengthy safety lecture we were off. The sky was blue and the sun was hot, but the water was cold. Jennifer started out slow, giggling at first because I was weighing down the back end. She then dared me to ride with no hands. I took that dare because, after all, how fast could she go? Well, I found out when she hit the gas, propelling me off the back and into the water.

I surfaced after a full submersion and looked around for the jet-ski so I could climb back on and get to shore before I caught the sniffles. "Good one, Jennifer" I thought, "Now come get me". Unfortunately she was nowhere to be seen. I attempted to call out for her but the shock of the cold water caused my voice to freeze (The water probably wasn't that cold, I was just being a wimp) and I couldn't yell. Then, I saw her; she was having a great time on the water, and didn't even seem to notice I was missing!

Now, I am not afraid of the water, I have always been an excellent swimmer, but it is what's in the water that makes me a little nervous. At times like that all the human mind seems to think about is the worst case scenario. I had watched *20,000 Leagues Under The Sea* a lot as a child and I remember fearing that giant squid: how it was coming to get me! I felt like there was a different sea beast brushing past my leg with every moment I waited perilously in the water (again, a wimp). I finally got my voice working and began calling out for Jennifer to come and save me.

After what seemed like an eternity she noticed I was missing, or decided she had time to come and retrieve me. I will never forget the huge smile on her face and the sound of her laughter as she pulled up next to me. She swore up and down she didn't know I was gone, and she would have come to get me sooner had she noticed, but I was not buying it. I climbed back on the jet-ski and we went back to shore. There was no way I was going to let her know I was worried, so I played it off perfectly macho but that was the last time I was going to let Jennifer Paulson give me a jet-ski ride.

TIME FOR A CHANGE

As Jennifer became a teenager she began to desire responsibility. She was becoming a person to be trusted and integrity was part of the foundation of her life. She was ready to be reliable, and begin her career in babysitting.

Jennifer's first job was to sit with her young cousin, Jordan, who was all boy and about one year old at the time. He was dropped off one afternoon and Jennifer was to be in charge. Of course, Nancy was there to offer her support and supervision, but it was Jennifer's show.

The afternoon went along as planned without any major mishaps. Jennifer cared for her cousin like a momma hen. Then, without warning, a certain aroma reached Jennifer's nostrils; she knew it was time for a change. She got out a new diaper, the baby wipes and placed her young cousin carefully on the couch and got to work cleaning him up. What happened next is both hilarious and mildly disturbing: the young boy began to squirm thus dumping the contents of the diaper onto the couch. Jennifer did not take this well and went into mild hysteria. She called out for her mom to come and rescue her, but Nancy assured her she could handle the situation and that Jennifer was on her own. After a few moments Jennifer collected herself, cleaned up the mess and her cousin was changed properly.

This event taught Jennifer a valuable child rearing lesson: when it comes to children, you need to get dirty to get clean.

RITE OF PASSAGE

Jennifer was involved in a program at Life Center known as Missionettes. This program was sponsored by the Assemblies of God and had many similarities to the Girls Scout organization. Missionettes was a discipleship program for young girls, teaching them to pursue the Lord and become strong women of God. The girls could earn badges for various accomplishments such as sewing, cooking, community involvement and Bible memorization. This program was right up Jennifer's alley.

The highest level of the program was Honor Star. It takes four years of serious dedication to achieve this status and many qualifications must be met. The Bible had to be read cover-to-cover and many verses needed to be memorized and recited. A young girl pursuing this status also needed to be involved in the community, serving in after-school programs, homeless shelters or in retirement homes. Church involvement was also a must. Helping in children's Sunday school classes or in other areas of church operation taught the girls what it meant to serve like Jesus served. The entire purpose of the program was to teach girls church involvement, the importance of community and Godly disciplines. Jennifer completed this program with flying colors, to the surprise of no one.

The Honor Star program was also a time of bonding and fellowship between mother and daughter. Nancy's heart swelled with pride as she watched her baby girl desire the things that God had for her, to publicly express her commitment to the community, church, and to the Lord. The program ended with a mother-daughter retreat and slumber party. It was just a time of rest, relaxation, and a time for mothers and daughters to be together.

When the Honor Star program comes to an end, Life Center holds a special ceremony in honor of every girl who completed the assignment, individually and as a group. It was a big to-do each year. The girls would wear pretty white dresses, get their hair done and wear a sparkling tiara and generally feel like a princess for the night. The girls would be center stage for the evening with all eyes on them. This accomplishment that Jennifer and the other girls around her made was quite a feat; one that most people who had served God for years might never accomplish. Being an Honor Star built a strong, Godly foundation for the lives of these young women. The girls were introduced individually by the director of the Honor Stars program, as they were escorted by their father to the front of the church sanctuary and were congratulated on their accomplishment by the entire church body and were celebrated in a reception following the ceremony. This was a rite of passage for these girls, moving into young womanhood. The Honor Star was not an easy task and not many girls could make it to the finish line. It was a road less traveled and as we all know, Jennifer always seemed to choose that road.

SAVE THE SLUGS

The friends we choose early in this life seem to shape who we are and who we become. If we choose wisely we will find success and our lives will prosper. If we choose poorly our lives will surely find misery and destruction. Jennifer made friends in her early years that would last a lifetime.

Early in her grade school years Jennifer made a dear friend who would become more of a sister than a friend; her name was Joellen Mcbee. Joellen was drawn to Jennifer immediately and since she was new to Life Christian Academy, needed a friend. Joellen could not help but fall in love with Jennifer's big smile (then covered in braces and headgear) and warm spirit. Joellen would give her a hard time about those braces and headgear when she wore them in school pictures that year. Jennifer simply claimed she was making a memory and that was that.

Throughout grade school they were average girls with an above average knack for silliness. They two of them, along with their dear friend Jessica White (back then she was Jessica Cleary), always seemed to have a joke between themselves that no one else understood. People around the school would smile and greet this group of girls as they walked through life together.

Jennifer, Joellen and Jessica (3 J's) all seemed to share the same convictions. All three of them were extraordinary students, were involved in extra-curricular activities, but still had time for antics. They all had a heart for creation, and at one point decided to put a stop to animal abuse. They set to work making signs, banners and hanging them around the school. The object of their cause: slugs. They would carry signs up and down the hall to advocate for these slimy creatures, not caring what others thought. Why slugs, you may ask? Who knows, the girls were young teens, who knows why they did anything!

BATH TIME

In her seventh grade year, Jennifer, along with about two dozen other classmates, had the opportunity to raise money and travel to our nation's capital. Along with her friends Joellen, Jessica and a few others, they left their parents behind for spring break. They were chaperoned by a few brave teachers and parents who didn't mind hyperactive teenagers. It was the first time Jennifer had been away from home by herself for that long, but it didn't bother her a bit (maybe it did Nancy). This was just the beginning of her world travels. She loved to explore and see new places near and far.

After a treacherous six and a half hour flight, with the only layover in Tennessee, the excited and exhausted classmates touched down in Washington D.C. The tour was off and running immediately as they were escorted to the Washington monument, a stone building constructed as a monument to our first president. Spring had just been born; the sky was clear and blue, but the air was cool and brisk. The students all took out their disposable camera's (not many parents trusted them with real ones) and captured the awe of this first monument.

During the fast paced and busy tour, Jennifer was able to visit some of our nation's most cherished and respected sights. Her class visited the Lincoln Memorial, the Museum of Flight and she caught a glimpse of the Wright brothers' first airplane. She visited the hallowed ground where President Abraham Lincoln was assassinated. Jennifer's jaw dropped as she went to the Mint where America's currency is printed. She shed a tear at the Vietnam memorial where are carved the names of over 55,000 soldiers who died defending our freedom. Two of her classmates were given the distinct honor of placing a wreath at the tomb of the unknown soldiers. Jennifer stood in line for hours as she waited for a tour of the White House. She even braved an unruly bum outside the Capital lawn. She took many pictures and gained many memories of our nation's symbols of freedom.

Although it was an amazing and educational trip, with her and all her friends there was sure to be some drama. Jennifer and almost a half dozen of her friends shared a single hotel room. You can only just imagine the antics. What happened to Jennifer to upset her I do not know (nor do I really want to), but she ended up in a flustered with her friends one night and decided to sleep in the bathtub. She took her blankets and pillows and went right to sleep in the comfort her own tub much to the amusement of her pals. Apparently she woke up the next morning with a sore back. Go figure.

THROW LIKE A GIRL

Jennifer also decided to give good, healthy competition a go when she was in Junior High. She tried out for basketball, softball and volleyball. Apparently she threw a softball like a girl, shot the basketball like an old lady, and the volleyball always seemed to go rogue whenever it came her way – and she would be the first to admit it! But she was in it for the laughs and memories. She, Joellen and Jessica made many memories on the bus trips to games; leaving school early, making errors and enjoying the fun of being with friends.

WHEN IT RAINS, IT POURS

At this stage in Jennifer's life, she began to develop a genuine relationship with the Lord. The teenage years were upon her and many choices and pressures would be thrown in her path. This world will discourage young girls with being satisfied with the way God made them, and much insecurity is born. Jennifer faced all of those same pressures, but it is how she responded that set her apart.

As Jennifer settled into her early teens she was faced with the divorce of her parents. Her world was split in two as everything she knew and counted on came crashing down. She had to choose where to live, and bitterness and anger knocked at the door of her soul. But through it all she never went off the deep end. She stayed in school and away from the behaviors normally associated with this type of domestic scenario. She kept her faith in God and He saw her through. The Lord was Jennifer's shepherd and He never left her side. This was an amazing testimony to those around her. She struggled of course, but kept her eyes above.

Today both her parents have remarried: Ken to Cindy and Nancy to Ned. Both marriages are healthy, happy and godly. This is another testament of God's healing and restoring power. Jennifer had great relationships with both parents and step-parents. Jennifer overcame.

JUST THE BEGINNING

Through the trials and tribulations of those hard years, God had a plan. He had a plan for the hurt and pain. Jennifer had to face the clouds and the storm, to see God's silver lining. As God was at work on Jennifer's heart, her eyes were opened to see those discarded and socially outcast young people in her circle of influence; those kids without the money to buy the fancy clothes, the social skills to fit in or a learning disability that had broken their spirit. Jennifer became that shoulder to cry on, and those open ears to listen. Her heart would break for those who didn't have the right tools to be the successful person God created them to be. This is what defined Jennifer; this was who she was becoming. She took her own struggles and the pain that her life brought, and turned them into strength for those she reached out to. This was shaping her adult life and ministry. That young girl with braces and headgear, who received her Honor Star, who threw like a girl and had many jet-skiing adventures, was becoming a woman of purpose and her purpose was just beginning.

Chapter Six

A Life Devoted
Years 16-20

Temptations and pressures are a part of the dealings of everyday life. Each man, woman and child must face both good and evil, success and destruction, life and death. Some will succumb to the worst of the fates and fall to death while others will resist that which is harmful and find life. The choice is ours, and the choice was Jennifer's.

The teenage years are some of the hardest years a human will go through. These years are full to the brim with those everyday choices both good and bad. Pressures are attacking from every angle: the media, peers, and even from within. These pressures at times might seem too difficult to withstand and the simplest choice may be to just fold under the pressure; but not for Jennifer. She withstood temptations, never falling into alcohol or drugs like so many teens do. She never entered into an immoral relationship with the opposite sex, but stayed pure throughout her entire life, saving herself for the man God had chosen for her. She never dated or had a steady boyfriend, not because she was undesirable or annoying, but because she wanted to have a whole heart without the baggage to give to that man.

Jennifer began to grow out of that young, awkward girl with head gear and braces. Her teeth were straight her eyes wide and blue and her hair was a soft brown. She had her first set of braces removed to rest up for the second pair she would get a year or so later. Her voice had changed from a little girl into that of a confident woman, even her walk had purpose. Every step was one step closer to God's ultimate plan for her; becoming a teacher.

THE HEARTBREAK GIRLS

Since Jennifer and her best pal Joellen went to different high schools, they would attend each other's school events. Jennifer went to the private school of Life Christian Academy and Joellen attended Henry Foss High School in Tacoma. The schools were separated by only a few blocks, and Joellen lived three houses down from Life Christian. The two still saw each other often. Football games, parties and even drivers education were shared together (can you imagine?). The two of them would pretty much do anything for a laugh.

Life Christian Academy didn't have traditional school dances, so Jennifer went with Joellen to the dances at Foss. The only problem was Jennifer was not a student and could only get in with a date, but this turned out not to be a problem. The two of them (mostly Joellen) would search Foss High School for the perfect boy to accompany Jennifer. Then once she was in the door she would promptly ditch her date and leave his heart broken in his chest. She did, however, pay him the courtesy of having pictures taken together. Jennifer of course had no intent of date-n-ditch, but she had to get in, right?

So if you're one of those boys and you're reading this, please laugh at the funny things girls do. I found it hard to believe at first as well. How could our dear, sweet Jennifer be a heartbreak girl? She really wasn't, she was just a teenage girl, and girls just want to have fun.

GUM WRAPPER ROMANCE

During one summer after her later years of high school, Jennifer went to a summer camp with Joellen and her church youth group. The normal activities for summer camp were involved: hiking, swimming, small groups, late night pranks and powerful Bible studies and worship services at night. There even was a little romance for Jennifer that year. A certain boy saw the spark in Jennifer's blue eyes and big wide smile. He became smitten by her beauty and did what any teenage boy would do in that situation: he followed her around like a little puppy dog.

This boy would just move from activity to activity, where ever Jennifer went. Young boys will do this when they have a crush on a girl, anything to just be in the same room with them. But this young boy went a step further: he got her a ring.......

Now stop right there mom and dad, not a diamond ring; a ring fashioned from the aluminum wrapper off a stick of chewing gum. He bent it and folded it with Jennifer in mind. He took meticulous care to be sure it was perfect and when he finally had it the way he wanted it, he took it and gave it to Jennifer as a token of his affections.

Jennifer was not interested in this boy and the crush was short lived; Joellen also did all she could to chase the boy away from her friend. But the heart and intentions behind the ring were innocent and it held a special place in Jennifer's heart. She kept the ring and it is still among her treasures to this day.

KEEPER OF FAMILY TREASURES

Memories of her ancestors and generations before her were very important to Jennifer. Where she came from and who paved the way for her to be born, was an integral part of who Jennifer was. She had a box filled with photos of her grandparents, aunts, uncles and cousins; she was the keeper of family treasures and took this responsibility quite seriously. She had older photographs of her grandma, Selma Paulson, before she was married; pictures of the motorcycles the Paulson's would sell at the turn of the century, and newspaper clipping of her father's four older brothers, as kids, sitting around a kitchen table, showcasing their mother's kitchen. The photo was taken in the early fifties before Ken was even born. Jennifer loved the memories of her family, and took the responsibility in her family of keeping these items safe and sacred.

FIRST OF MANY

The memory of receiving our driver's license for the first time and our first car are memories we both cherish and cringe at as we get older; the drudgery of driver's education, the nervous stomach of our driver's test, and the feeling of freedom and emancipation in our first solo drive. We owned the road and we could go anywhere at any time, as long as we were home by curfew.

As mentioned earlier, Jennifer took her driver's education at Foss High School with her pal Joellen. How the two of them made it through class without giggling and being asked to leave is anyone's guess, but they did. Jennifer earned her license before most of the students in her class because she was born in the summer, thus being a few months older. This made Jennifer the new Life Christian Academy mascot: the chauffer.

Jennifer received her first car shortly after she received her license, her first of many cars. This car stood out among other things because of the paint: it was spray paint. The car was a matte red Hyundai Excel. This fact didn't bother Jennifer in the slightest; she was becoming independent. She would leave her dad's home in University Place and travel five miles or so to Life Christian. On the way she would stop and pick up a few friends who lived close by. Many mishaps would happen along the way from running out of gas to an overheated radiator. Unfortunately, this meant they never made it to school on time. Ken had to write a note every day. He finally got wise and just photocopied the same note every day, and just changing the date as needed.

In the end they did make it to school every day and Jennifer was still at the top of her class (surprised?). She was young and would only be that way for a short time. The memories of driving to school in that spray painted car were memories she, and her friends, always cherished and still do to this day.

FATHER KNOWS BEST

Mortality is not a concept understood by many teenagers. They many times feel they are invincible – some more than others. They feel they have it all figured out and their grasp on the world does not need the input of bothersome parents telling them how to live. Now, Jennifer was a well-behaved teen to say they least, but she did however have her moments.

During high school Jennifer and her brother Mark lived with their dad in an apartment in University Place. The four-plex was set back off the main road through the city and sat up on a slight hill. Directly off the living room was a balcony overlooking the driveway where the family parked their cars (the spray painted one too). Jennifer had just earned her driver's license and shouted through the open door to the balcony that she was going to run an errand. Ken asked her if she had her license on her. Jennifer replied she left it in her room but was only going down the street and she didn't need it. Her dad insisted she get it but Jennifer continued to resist thinking it was a silly to walk all the way up the stairs and retrieve the license – but the battle between father and daughter continued. After being threatened with restriction, she began to consider giving in.

It was a hard thing for Jennifer, or any teen for that matter, but in the end she succumbed to her father's request. She went upstairs to her room and stuffed her license into her pocket. She smiled at her dad as she drove down the road to the drug store.

When we are young we don't seem to grasp the fact that our parents do know best, if only because they have made more mistakes than we have. They have seen the cause and effect of choices made both for good and bad. When we are older and have children of our own, we understand the reasoning behind our parents supposed strict rules. It is so we don't make the mistakes and suffer the consequences they did.

A few minutes later Jennifer returned from her errand, pulling up to the apartment in her spray painted car. This time she had tears streaming down her cheeks. When her dad asked what happened she had no choice but to admit it: she was pulled over by a police officer. She ended up not getting a ticket but she may very well have if she didn't have her license in her pocket. Jennifer learned a valuable lesson through this; another universal truth: Father still knows best.

THE DOG ATE MY GAS

Family vacations and road trips can be some of our favorite memories. The anticipation and excitement before the trip begins, the thrill of the journey to our destination, and the fun of actually living out the dreams we had months before. Wherever the destination, no matter who we take with us, these are some of our most fun-filled memories.

The Paulson family getaways were no different. Jennifer's uncles, cousins and immediate family would trek out to Bank's Lake in Eastern Washington for some fun on the water. Tents would be erected, water sport equipment would be unloaded and the cooler would be stocked. Let the fun begin!

On many trips, Jennifer would bring a friend along since the men greatly outnumbered the women. They would have great fun in conversation, around the campfire and on the water. The girls would share a tent and I'm sure keep others around them awake at night with their giggling and talking.

On one particular summer excursion, Jennifer and her friend Carmin decided to take the jet-ski out for a ride on the lake. They strapped on their life jackets (probably those same yellow ones with the blue straps) and set out for an adventure. The rest of the camp went about their day making a fire, cooking meals and playing around the campground. Time passed and Jennifer and her friend had not yet returned. After a search of the lake and surrounding campsites one of Jennifer's cousins had to grab another jet-ski and go out on the lake and track them down.

Finally, Jennifer and her friend appeared and drove their jet-ski up to the shore with big smiles on their faces. Jennifer then had to explain to her dad that they ran out of gas on the middle of the lake. They were not paying attention to the gas meter and before they knew it, the ride came to a halt.

Now rumor has it that Jennifer and her pal had to abandon the jet-ski and swim to shore. They had to find someone to give them some gas (from the story she told me, it was some teenage boys) and drive them out to the middle of the lake to fill up. Now imagine for a moment swimming to shore from the middle of a busy lake in the middle of summer: boats and water-skiers zooming by – rather dangerous if you ask me. But Jennifer was fearless and always ready for another adventure.

GETTING AHEAD

If the word Jennifer Ann Paulson were in the dictionary, the meaning would be: to excel in all things pursued. As she was coming to the end of her teen years and her high school graduation was fast approaching, she began to prepare for college. Life Christian Academy offered advanced placement courses for excelling students who wanted a jump start on earning college credit. Needless to say, Jennifer was on board. She would take on this extra work load in order to get ahead. She knew where she was going and could see the steps ahead of her. It was a long uphill climb but when the goal was set, nothing could dishearten her.

Jennifer graduated from high school in June of 1998. She graduated with honors and walked the platform in her white robe with a blue and red tassel. This was not only a graduation from high school, but a rite of passage to the next stage of her life. She already had a few leads on different colleges interested in having her attend their university. Pacific Lutheran University had even offered her a chance to join a scholarship program. Her dad had graduated from this very school with a degree in business and she would have been honored to attend, but it wasn't the right choice for her. She ended up enrolling at Seattle Pacific University. She had her sights set on a degree in education. Over the course of her five year stint with S.P.U. she would change her major and minor to fit the calling on her life that came into focus more and more as her life journey continued. She was beginning the final steps of her greatest adventure yet: fulfilling God's plan.

DIVINE DEVOTION

The Bible says that in our God there is no changing or shifting of shadow; that He is the same yesterday, today and forever. God has a plan for each of us and salvation is an eternal hope for all who put their trust in His son Jesus Christ. Jesus paid for our sins with His life; we do not have to carry the burden of the things in our lives that cause us guilt or hold us back from God. We simply need to become humble, admit our wrong doing and ask for forgiveness. That's it!

Jennifer accepted this salvation and pursued a personal relationship with God. She would spend time everyday reading the Bible and praying for different situations in her life. Instead of carrying the burdens of life, she gave them to God to carry for her. Her faith became stronger and stronger as she would commit the Word of God to memory. God was alive to her and in her heart and life. She had no doubts about her salvation or destiny. Each day as she would dig deeper in God's Word for truth and God would open her eyes to more clearly see the path in front of her.

That, dear reader is the key to a fulfilling life: following God's guidance. Many people follow their own map and their own course of action and some may find success. But when they are outside of God's ultimate plan, there is a lack of peace and fulfillment. Each person on earth is created for a very specific purpose. God uses the situations of our lives and the environment we were born into to mold us into that person He created us to be. God has a plan for everyone. Orphans in Africa, AIDS victims, convicts in prison, homosexuals, people who have had sex-change operations – they all have a destiny: salvation.

Jennifer would not have been the person she was without her personal relationship with God. She made time to seek Him everyday, journaling what she learned and listening for the still small voice of the Lord. She learned to shut down her busy mind and be still so God could speak to her heart. He led and she followed. Her life became in perfect balance with God's eternal plan and she began to race toward the finish line; taking with her along her journey, as many as would follow.

Chapter Seven

A Life Devoted
Years 21-30

Jesus Christ was a man of many passions. He was passionate for His Father's house, the lost souls around Him, and for children. He taught that the Kingdom of Heaven is for such as them and the Bible says that out of the mouths of infants He ordained praise. A child is filled with faith and wonder as they look at all God has created around them. They don't try to rationalize God or shove Him inside of a home made box; they accept Him at His word.

Jesus was also a teacher. He spoke in parables, making biblical principals come to life through stories that people could relate to. He used examples of crops, land, cattle and money. He related to where people were at, and explained it for them to understand. He would be very stern at times in His teaching, but He needed to get the point across.

Faith was not only something Jesus taught, but something He lived. Two sisters (Mary and Martha) sent word to Jesus reporting that their brother, and a friend of Jesus, had passed away. The sisters had placed him in a tomb and began to grieve heavily. When Jesus arrived He told the sisters to have faith and they would see the glory of God. Jesus lifted His eyes to heaven and called out to His heavenly Father. He then called into the tomb and their brother was raised from the dead.

Jennifer's life was a life of faith. She believed that people did not have to stay dead in their sins but could be resurrected into new life. She would lift her own head to heaven and call on the heavenly Father for the strength to guide people out of the grave that their sins had dug for them. She knew beyond the shadow of a doubt that as long as our faith is in Christ, we would never truly die.

HOLD THE PHONE

Often times Jennifer would become inspired by the infusion of fresh new ideas. She once read a magazine article stating that some people can become such great friends that they can stop a phone conversation mid-sentence, hang up, and then pick up the conversation a few days later, without missing a beat. She decided to put this theory to the test. She called up her buddy Jessica and explained to her the experiment. Jessica wasn't sure it would work and tried her best to explain the reasoning behind her theory when….CLICK. Jennifer had hung up. Naturally, Jessica was beside herself with hysteria. She called Jennifer back only to receive a reprimand that they needed to stick to the project. The two kept the procedure going for a few days and finally realizing it was too hard to remember the conversation the next day.

The two friends would spend many hours on the phone (this I remember from our childhood). They never seemed to run out of things to talk about and if they did, they would just talk about nothing; apparently girls can do that kind of thing! They even shared an earthquake while on the phone together. No matter what the conversation, these two genuinely loved each other, cared about each other's lives and genuinely couldn't spend enough time together.

DON'T BUG ME

Jennifer and Jessica had a lot of fun together growing up and were as close as sisters. They had been friends since they were nine when Jennifer asked if Jessica was related to Beverly Cleary, the famous children's author. Slumber parties were always on their agenda even as adults. Apparently Jennifer walked and talked in her sleep but that's another story altogether. They would spend a lot of time camping and had many adventures on the water. If it was fun, Jennifer was always on board. She loved cliff jumping and punching the throttle on the jet-ski. Jessica was a little bit more reserved, and Jennifer loved to push her to the boundaries.

During one fun summer vacation the two of them had spent the day on the beach of Lake Chelan. They had been camping and took a nighttime walk down to the water. It must have been muggy that night because there were many bugs flying around the girls' heads. The two were getting annoyed and Jessica suggested Jennifer just turn on the flashlight and shoo them away. Jennifer did so only to be greeted, in midair, by a big, hairy, black bat. Needless to say, much screaming ensued as the two friends bolted down the beach towards light and to safety.

MEMORIES OF A TEACHER

Jennifer always had a lasting impact on everyone she came into contact and interacted with. She may not have been a teacher's pet in school but she was definitely a favorite and was always memorable. One of her High School teachers, Mr. Stan Seeley, had some heartfelt memories of Jennifer and I will share them with you now:

I knew Jennifer from the time she was born because of the church and being a friend of the family. However, it was not until she was a student at Life Christian Academy in my anatomy and physiology classes that I really got to know her as a student and as a friend. I have taught for 48 years and have instructed over 12,000 students so when I compare Jennifer it is to that large of a group. Jennifer's strongest aptitude was not science and yet because she maximized her potential like few students I have ever had, she was at the highest level. She was always pleasant and never had a discipline problem. Beyond that she was compassionate to other less capable students and was always ready to help them.

After her high school graduation I followed her career at Seattle Pacific University through periodic visits at church. We were able to share brief prayers together about a variety of things, whether school challenges or needs among family and friends. It is noteworthy that she was always more concerned with others than about herself.

When I found out Jennifer had followed in my footsteps as a teacher, I was obviously pleased, because I could see that her abilities and personal qualities were going to have a significant impact on all the students God brought to her classroom. Teachers are investors in the lives of others and their greatest joy comes in seeing that their investments are growing. I can say that of all my students, Jennifer Paulson was making some of the greatest returns on my small investment into her life the brief time she was given. This story doesn't end on a note of sadness because at this very moment she is reaping the greatest rewards of a life well lived. She is in the presence of her Lord and Savior hearing His words: "Well done, my good and faithful servant."

Jennifer's life was guided and instructed by people who genuinely cared about the plan God had for her life. Like Mr. Seeley stated: A teacher is an investor. They give all they have for the sake of someone else in hopes that their stock will grow and flourish. It is because of people like this and a string of many others, that Jennifer became who she was.

PAULIEY WANT A MILKSHAKE?

During her college years Jennifer also made some great new friends – Jenniey and Jill. Jenniey felt that too many girls at their university were named Jenny, so she "renamed" Jennifer. She took the "Paul" from Paulson, and added "iey" from her own name and the two of them started calling Jennifer "Pauliey."

Jill and Pauliey were very close in college and even spent time working in the cafeteria together. Pauliey was convinced that washing dirty dishes for hours on end would be tons of fun and a great memory they would share together later on in life. Apparently, the dishwashing stint lasted an entire quarter, but good old' Pauliey just couldn't find the downside, even after she got a staph infection from a pair of unwashed gloves. Rumor has it that the two of them survived on shakes made from ice cream and peanut butter cups. So *that's* where the enthusiasm for dishwashing came from: sugar!

STATUE OF LIBERTY

Let's be honest now, Jennifer was a typical young adult, and aside from her selfless persona and caring attitude, she was still young and free. She always wanted to do the right thing but from time to time things might go a little bit astray. Like the night she went out to a nightclub, and snuck an underage girl in with her.....

Don't fret Ken and Nancy. Take a deep breath; it's not as bad as it sounds. It was her dear friend Jenniey's 21st birthday, and Jennifer (Pauliey), the birthday girl and Jill wanted to go out to a nightclub in Pioneer Square. Only one problem: Jill was not 21 years old yet. No problem for Jennifer- she simply borrowed a driver's license from a friend who looked like Jill, put on her pink vinyl pants and they were ready for a night on the town.

The plan was executed perfectly as they ran into no hassles from the bouncers and the party began. They all sat up at the bar feeling very adult and grown up, but after one drink the lightweights that never drank felt like they had had enough. They sat outside on the curb and waited patiently for a taxi. The bouncers didn't like the loitering and yelled at the ladies to move. So Jennifer led the posse into a waiting taxi (unfortunately it belonged to someone else but Jennifer just kind snuck into it before anyone could stop them).

Now this is where the story gets good and those of you who knew Jennifer best knew she was not a drinker at all. She felt it wasn't worth the trouble, money or the calories but this night she would make her mark in the drinking world. There is a drink called the "Statue of Liberty," where you take your shot, dip your fingers in it, light them on fire and hold them up like Lady Liberty as you down your shot; then extinguish the flames out in your mouth. None of the girls had the guts to attempt this feat – except for our Jennifer.

They had taken the taxi to a friend's home for a visit and it was there that she was presented with the challenge. Like an old pro she dipped, she ignited, she downed and she extinguished. This may have been the only time in her life that Jennifer would drink, but she made it a memorable event.

HONORABLE MENTION

Jennifer was always creating memorable moments no matter where she was or who she was with. Apparently, she got a cut on her hand during lunch out with some friends. This does not seem out of the ordinary, except she got the cut from her paper napkin. How she did this was anyone's guess and after she told the waiter, he sent his co-workers by the table to witness this amazing feat. Not much more to say about a paper napkin cut, but it did deserve honorable mention.

THE EUROPEAN ADVENTURE

God has made His people so diverse in every way; in their architecture, language, foods and culture. God celebrates our differences and we should too. Jennifer has always loved to travel, and the summer after she graduated from college she was blessed with the opportunity to travel around Europe with Sarah, her roommate the last year of college, and a few other girlfriends. And knowing Jennifer, she was going to travel for as little money as humanly possible.

The ladies decided to meet up in Paris at the *Arc de Triomphe*, a massive monument built in the early 1800's to honor those who fought and died in the French Revolution. Jennifer had no cell phone and she didn't know much French at all, but still managed to smile her way to their rendezvous point where they would consider their next course of action and take in the sights of the city. This is where the adventure of a lifetime would begin.

The mission statement of the trip was simple: To see as much of Europe as possible, for as little money as possible. This was fine with Jennifer; her plan was to stay the night in hostels. Although it sounds like something out of a horror movie, a hostel is basically a dorm room with a few bunks, a chair and maybe a toilet.

The ladies would travel from city to city by train. Most countries in Europe use the Euro so changing money was not an issue. They traveled to Munich, Germany; to Rome, Italy; to Prague, in the Czech Republic and to London, England. They stayed a few days in the Italian Riviera and gorged themselves on gelato; relaxing by the water. They were able to see the Coliseum in Rome, the very place where Christians were executed from 80 A.D. when its construction was completed. This trip was a great opportunity for Jennifer to experience this world that God made for us.

THE LADY IN THE LEOPARD SPOTTED HEELS

Jennifer always had a knack for saving a dollar. Most people who know the family claim; it comes from her dad. But in any case, during the European adventure, Jennifer would always be on the lookout for the cheapest hostels to rent for that night. During their stay in Germany, Jennifer heard about a five dollar a night hostel and couldn't resist. The ladies tracked it down and truthfully were not shocked at all to find it was nothing but a big tent where they had to sleep lying on a mat in the dirt. The others were probably not too happy about this, but knowing Jennifer, I'm sure she thought it was great.

As they got off the train in the Czech Republic a flashy lady with leopard printed high heel shoes came up to them, not speaking much English but claimed she had a place to stay. Jennifer and the others were not too happy with the price that was quoted and dismissed the woman. A few minutes later, our Jennifer felt that she could talk the lady down in price and bolted into the crowd of the busy station. How she found that woman again was beyond any one of the ladies, but she did, and the price was dropped. Unfortunately you get what you pay for and the place they stayed was later described as the worst place a human could sleep. All thanks to the lady with the leopard printed heels.

A GROWING FAMILY

During Jennifer's twenties a few more women were added to the Paulson clan. Ken was married in 2005 to a wonderful brunette named Cindy Klein. The two were wed at Life Center in Gray's Chapel. Jennifer was a bridesmaid and was very happy her father found a woman that made him happy and a woman that loved God. Nancy had also married years prior to Ned Heisler and Ned brought with him his four sons.

The following year her brother Mark married a dazzling blonde named Rebecca (Becky) Powers. The two met on a semi-blind date and have been together ever since. They also were married at Life Center surrounded by excited parents. Jennifer was also a bridesmaid and was thrilled for her brother, but also overjoyed to finally have a sister. A few years went by and

Mark and Becky welcomed a beautiful, healthy baby girl into the world: Savannah Paulson. She is blonde and with blue eye and is growing by leaps and bounds.

URBAN PROMISE

In 1988, Christian Speaker and sociologist Dr. Tony Campolo felt the call to seek justice for the impoverished and liberation for those who have become oppressed. He felt these convictions so strongly that he formed the Evangelical Association for the Promotion of Education or E.A.P.E. This ministry gave birth to Urban Promise. Urban Promise had one mission and one mission only: to equip children and teens with skills necessary for achievement, life management, spiritual growth and leadership rooted in the principals of Christian faith.

Jennifer attended a meeting at Seattle Pacific University and heard Dr. Campolo speak and couldn't sign up fast enough. This was right up her alley. During her summer off she traveled to Wilmington, Delaware where Urban Promise ministered. Jennifer was definitely in her element and believed very strongly in the mission of Urban Promise. The director would recall years later of the leadership by servanthood Jennifer would display.

Those who volunteered noticed a spark about Jennifer, a light behind those big blue eyes that gave her passion for a community that she didn't even live in, and for its children. She always seemed to walk in a way that commanded respect; not by being overbearing, but by walking in humility. They would put on outreaches in the community, offering after school and day care. She poured out her life for those children, tutoring them in academics and social skills. She would go to tougher parts of town without any fear, because they needed hope too.

The staff lived on the ministry grounds and were assigned to various ministries depending on their individual callings and gifts. During the summer it was more of a camp setting. The normal activities were available but also with tutoring and Bible study sessions. The staff acted as counselors and were in charge of a group of kids.

During one of Jennifer's two stays in Wilmington, a teen came into the program with a tremendous amount of emotional baggage. He suffered from being bi-polar, suicidal and all that comes with the mixture. He was angry at the world and would threaten and even assault staff. Concerned for their safety, they were preparing to dismiss this teen – until Jennifer stepped in.

Jennifer had a reputation for having drawing a positive response from people just by walking into the room or even from the sound of her voice.

Those around her knew whose she was and what she stood for: Christ. Her heart was pure and strong and like we have seen in the past, full of compassion for those hurting.

Jennifer began to reach out to this teen and he became calm and his angry outbursts began to subside. He began to open up to her serenity and would share with her about the troubles of his life and his struggles. By the end of the summer, this formerly angry and violent teen had accepted the forgiveness of Jesus Christ into his heart, and his life was forever impacted by Jennifer Paulson.

Urban Promise was a solid training ground for Jennifer's future work. She was known for her virtue, patience, persistence and leadership. Her heart would break for the young people of Wilmington and she was brought to tears during her final staff meeting, feeling she could have done more for the community. But her work there was done. It was time to pass the torch. She came to Urban Promise to impact the community; little did she know the community would impact her.

PULLING OUT THE BIG GUNS

Teaching was more than a job for Jennifer, it was a passion. She felt responsible for the future of each student and she took this very seriously. Going the extra mile to cheer up a student or staying after class for an extra tutoring session was a normal part of her day. Jennifer began to care deeply for each student placed under her care. She became their mentor, instructor and their friend. Although she was having the time of her life and in the center of God's plan, her heart would grow heavy for her students. During her first year of teaching at a Middle School, many of the children she taught didn't have books available to take home and study. This broke her heart that her students didn't have the resources to pursue their valuable education. She began to petition the Tacoma Public School where she was working at the time, for books that the children could take home; but to no avail. Her heart would weigh heavier and heavier and many times she would weep with friends and family at what she felt was an injustice. Then she figured enough was enough. She pulled out the big guns: she called Dad!

Ken Paulson supported his daughter in her cause, so he would attend every School Board meeting constantly petitioning them with a request for books to take home. Both Ken and Jennifer felt the students should be treated as equals, not as a minority. Finally, after months of persistence and pestering, the students had their take-home text books.

This story is not meant to put the school system down in any way;

Tacoma has some of the best schools in the state. But what it shows is the dedication Jennifer had for her students; and Ken had to see his daughter succeed. She was an advocate for their futures and she would not take no for an answer.

MEMORY OF A COLLEAGUE

Jennifer was admired for her dedication and sweet spirit by so many of her co-workers. She was an amazing example to all of them, even those who had been teaching for decades. I have a letter written concerning Jennifer's life and career, written by a fellow teacher at the school where Jennifer passed away. I share it with you now:

I had the great pleasure of teaming with Jennifer for the 2008-10 school years. Jennifer was the LRC (Learning Resource Center) teacher and I was the speech therapist and we shared approximately 15 students (who received both LRC and speech therapy).

Jennifer had many responsibilities as the LRC teacher. In addition to the typical special ed teacher responsibilities: providing daily instruction to children, meeting with parents, serving as the "host" for weekly Teacher Support Team and Student Response Teams, teaming with teachers to plan interventions, etc., Jennifer also took on a host of extra responsibilities, always with a big smile. Jennifer signed up for extra committees and took advantage of any/all trainings that she felt would enrich her ability to provide innovative, motivating, and productive instruction.

Jennifer was so pleased when she completed her Master's Degree in spring of 2009. She commented that now she would have time for her friends who she felt she neglected during her graduate work. She had just completed the final phase of her special education certificate at the time of her death. I had the privilege of being one of the advisors for her certification project. I was so very impressed with her efficient organization and execution of her required work. I learned so much when reviewing her certification notebooks.

Jennifer almost always stood outside her door each morning and each afternoon to greet all students when entering and leaving. They got used to her big welcoming smiles and "hello's" and "goodbye's". She made a point of seeking out students in the hall who needed and extra connection or stroke from an adult. She was quick to help any Kindergartener or first grader struggling with a backpack, locker or untied shoe. Jennifer and I had many IEP (Individual Education Plan) meetings together. Jennifer was the advisor for these shared students so took the "lead" in the parent meetings. Jennifer did an amazing job of making the parents (and students if they attended) feel comfortable. She moved through the pages of the IEP with care, checking frequently to make sure the parents understood and provided clarification and examples when needed. We often needed an interpreter, since many of our students families spoke Spanish (and occasionally other languages such as Russian or Vietnamese). Jennifer did a wonderful job of orchestrating the complicated responses, questions and clarifications needed in these cases.

Jennifer always made families feel that their child was special and valued. She stressed the students' strength. Jennifer had a very kind, gentle way of explaining students' learning challenges and deficits. She worked hard to help parents understand the homework and how they could help their student at home. Parents were never made to feel rushed. When anyone met with Jennifer, be it student, parent, guardian, or staff member, she made that person feel like they were her top priority and gave them her full and undivided attention. She was the consummate team member for families, staff and students.

Jennifer loved the challenge of "special" students. I never once saw her express frustration or discouragement and very often saw her go the extra mile to figure out how to solve a difficult behavioral or learning challenge. Jennifer was quick to request the help of specialists when needed. She appreciated the input of anyone who could help her meet her students' needs in the most efficient and positive way. Jennifer went out of her way so often, for example, one student had an oral-sensory disability and ate very little, and definitely very little that was healthy. Jennifer incorporated a snack time into her LRC for this student and others in the group, slowly and gently introducing a variety of foods this student had not previously tolerated. Often special-ed teachers get frustrated or "burned" out with particular students, especially those with behavior challenges. Jennifer did the opposite. She relished those students…always making them feel appreciated and safe and going the extra mile to provide them with unique and individual supports. Jennifer also did a great job teaming with general education teachers with whom she shared her students. She kept the communication lines wide open so she knew how her students were doing in their other classes and the teachers knew how they were doing in their LRC classes.

Jennifer was very mature beyond her years. She always put others first. She was the perfect example of consideration, always asking what would "work" for the other person and always volunteering to do more than her share of joint projects. Jennifer came to school early and stayed late. It was so evident that her work and students were a passion for her.

Jennifer was loved by her students and staff. She was "the person" for many of her more needy students, the one adult in their lives they could count on for help and support. She was truly a person who lived a Christ-like life, walking the walk of a loving, giving and gentle person, always setting an exemplary model for others.

The staff and students will truly miss Jennifer and continue to keep her *memory alive. She made our school a better place and touched the lives of so many, enriching them by shining her examples of hard work, love, perseverance, respect, and selflessness.*

I miss Jennifer so very much. I think of her many times each week. I will never forget her big smile and her amazing gifts as a teacher. I miss her friendship as well as her partnership in teaching. I think of Jennifer's family each week also, and hold them close in prayer. I know how proud they must be of her and how much their hearts must hurt as they feel her absence.

I have children Jennifer's age and as they marry, begin families, tackle graduate programs, develop in their careers and interests, take vacations, volunteer in our community and abroad, grow in the Lord, etc., I think of Jennifer; she was doing many of these things, an amazing person the same age as my dear ones; a dear one too, who is with God now, taken from us too soon, and missed so much by so many here on earth.

LEAP OF FAITH

It is an empowering feeling, dear reader, knowing the exact reason you are put here on this earth. You will walk with purpose, direction and confidence and you will no longer waste time with tasks and relationships that contain no significance for God's ultimate purpose. So many of us have dreams and goals for our lives, but at times we feel they are out of reach. But they can be obtained and more easily than one might think.

It starts with commitment to the Lord and giving Him control of your life. The Bible says that God will give you the desires of your heart, and it is true, but our heart is wicked and full of sin. So we ask Him to put His pure desires inside our hearts, not asking Him to grant our selfish purposes. Then they will be fulfilled, for they will be His.

If we have learned anything from Jennifer Ann Paulson, it is to just be open; to make our lives accessible to God. Do not be afraid to take a leap of faith like she did, putting her life and heart in the line of fire. God will grant us more satisfaction and fulfillment than we could ever come up with on our own. Jennifer was ready, willing and able to move forward with God's plan and as she unknowingly reached the end of her days, she continued to look forward to the future that God had for her and to be prepared for what was coming next.

SECOND INTERLUDE

The Bible says to love your enemy as yourself and bless those who persecute you. This is easier said than done. But Jesus set the example for us. Many times during His ministry people tried to take His life. They tried to push Him off a cliff, they tried countless times to have Him arrested and they accused Him of being possessed by the devil. All the while, those who mocked Him and accused Him, were the people He came to save. He came to seek and save that which was lost. Jennifer followed this example for her entire life; she would seek out the lost. She went out of her way and gave up her time to find those in need of salvation.

Over the years after Jennifer graduated from Seattle Pacific University, the same young man she befriended in that school cafeteria began to seek Jennifer out. He would call her countless times and even went as far as to show up at her school. An unhealthy obsession was being birthed in this young man, but Jennifer being the follower of Christ that was would handle these situations with grace. She explained that his behavior was inappropriate and therefore unacceptable. Then she would send him on his way. She then filed an anti-harassment order that prohibited this young man from contacting her.

A year went by and in December 2009 he showed up at the school where our Jennifer was working. Jennifer called the police, but by the time they showed up at the school, he was gone.

The following February 19th, he waited outside the school in his car and began to follow Jennifer as she left for the day. She noticed him following her and promptly called 911. The operator instructed her to drive to nearest police station and that's exactly what she did. He followed her and was arrested on the spot for violating the anti-harassment order that had been filed in the fall of 2008.

A sigh of relief was breathed by Jennifer and her family. This had done it; this young man was finally gone. The family figured the arrest would change his mindset and he would no longer be bothering Jennifer. She could go about living her life without the anxiety of this young man showing up again. Her family could rest easy, believing Jennifer was now safe. Unfortunately, this peace was short lived.

The following Monday this young man made bail and was released from the Pierce County jail. One of Tacoma's fine police officers contacted

Jennifer out of concern to let her know of his release. Jennifer and her family again were on high alert. Jennifer handled it very wisely and stayed at her mother's house for that first night. During her stay she asked her mom and step-dad to join with her in prayer for this young man. They prayed that God would touch his heart, heal his wounds and set him on the path to destiny.

As the week went by Jennifer continued to go to work. Nothing would hold her back from being with her students. She had meetings that week after hours and even had her room set up for a student's birthday on Friday morning. Jennifer was in the epicenter of God's plan and she knew she couldn't step outside of it. Her heart was filled with God's peace and love. Her faith was at its strongest and she was ready to see Jesus face to face.

The morning of February 26 began like any other day. Jennifer got up, readied herself for school and set out for work. She met up with a fellow teacher that morning and they walked from the parking lot to the school together. The sky was a bit gray with the slightly overcast sky. The two women began to approach the school and suddenly, in the blink of an eye, their world changed forever.

Three gunshots were heard piercing the morning air. A woman's scream filled the morning with unease. Tears began to flow, hearts were broken and lives were torn in two during that moment. The same young man who Jennifer had befriended in the cafeteria those many years ago, the same young man Jennifer believed in, the same young man who Jennifer prayed for, had approached from the bushes outside of the school, pointed a gun at our dear Jennifer, and had pulled the trigger.....

Part 3: Love

"…..and Love. But the greatest of these is Love."
1 Corinthians 13:13

From the Journal of Jennifer Ann Paulson:

8-26-08
Lord,
* I thank You so much for the blessings You have bestowed on me. Somehow I have a <u>good</u> reputation in the Tacoma School District and at University of Washington Tacoma. During student teaching, I seriously questioned whether or not I could ever be a teacher. My success is all yours- <u>Thank you!</u> Please help me to make the most of it and bless others for you. Please help me to LOVE my students!*

Dear Jenny,

Where do I even begin? Amekhi (my son) started Kindergarten and you would be so proud of him! I would've sent you pictures on his first day of school looking so handsome in his tie for chapel. I decided to send him to a Christian school just like we went to. He has already memorized two Bible verses. Do you remember how we memorized a million verses in 8th grade and we would all carry around note cards with them on it? I thank God everyday that I went to Life Christian Academy and met you in third grade. Who would think?? Who would think that two goofy girls would remain such close friends? Neither of us had sisters, so I think God planned it that way, you know. Not having you in my life has left a huge void in my heart. My sweet friend and sister in Christ, what am I to do now? Life was supposed to be shared with you. We were supposed to continue to pray together, encourage one another, and be each others biggest cheerleader!

Oh, Jenny, I miss you like crazy! Not a day has gone by that I don't think about you or the impact you had on my life. My heart knows that you are in such a glorious place; surrounded with joy, freedom, and love in heaven. But I can't help the tears streaming down my face as I remember the freedom I found being with you. Grace abounded in every conversation that we had, allowing me to grow or make mistakes. You introduced me to Beth Moore, and I introduced you to Kim Walker and Misty Edwards. You gently pushed me to overcome some major weaknesses in my life, and I would pray with you for your kids at school. Oh how I miss you! Even in the midst of knowing that God is good all the time, I crave our friendship something desperate. You are a gem, a shining star, and your purity in lifestyle is something to admire and strive for. Every time I hear "Focus on the Family", I think of you. Every time I read a political article I know exactly how you would respond. Every time I am in a special education meeting, I think of the school systems loss of a woman with the utmost integrity. You have invoked in me a deeper sense of compassion and empathy; not in your death but in your life! All I can say is THANK YOU for loving me. THANK YOU for never giving up on me, and THANK YOU for being Jesus' conduit of love in my life. I adore you Jennifer Ann Paulson and you'll be the first person I look for when I join the glory of heaven! I am glad that we'll have an eternity to continue our friendship when it temporarily stopped here on earth. Death cannot destroy the bond that God created!

In Him,
Your best friend and sister in Christ,
Joellen McBee

Chapter Eight

A Life Celebrated

Eternity Begins

Certain moments in history have a way of becoming permanently burned into our memories. We remember exactly where we were, what we were doing and who we were with at the point we heard the news: September 11, 2001, the assassination of John F. Kennedy, the earthquake in the Bay Area in the late 80's or the fall of the Berlin Wall. These moments are frozen into our memories and imprinted on our mind's eye. When we return to those moments our hearts become filled with emotion and it seems like just yesterday these events took place. For those of us in the greater Tacoma area, and anyone who knew Jennifer Ann Paulson, we will remember where we were the moment they heard the horrifying news: Jennifer was gone.

THE CALM BEFORE THE STORM

The afternoon before our dear Jennifer passed away, she was in school tending to her students as she always did. She was filled with joy as she instructed each one of them in the area where she wanted to see them excel. Success is contagious! Jennifer had found it, and she desired to pass it on to her students.

In between classes, toward the end of the day, one of her fellow teachers passed Jennifer in the hall as she was escorting her students to class. An overwhelming feeling over took this teacher at that moment. She saw Jennifer, like a momma duck with her students following behind her, with a glowing radiance. It seemed like someone had lit a light in Jennifer's chest and that light was pouring out of every part of her body. God's love was so strong in Jennifer's life at that moment it could be seen with the physical eye. Her smile was at its brightest and a peace rested upon Jennifer in that moment. This teacher noted the beauty she saw in Jennifer; a supernatural beauty and kept it in her heart. Jennifer was a child of the Most High God and in the exact center of His plan.

Jennifer just smiled and waved, continuing to class with her precious students in tow. This moment stuck with that certain teacher as the events of the next day unfolded and the community was thrust into confusion. What she saw was like calm before the storm; almost like God knew what was coming.

CONFIRMED

I will always remember the morning of February 26, 2010, as will hundreds of others who knew and loved Jennifer. As I drove to work that morning I heard that a woman had been shot in front of a school in Tacoma, but all that really registered was the fact no children were hurt. That was a relief. I got to the jobsite and went about my morning with not an inkling of what had really happened.

Around ten a.m. I received a phone call from a good friend and he gave me the news: Jennifer Paulson had passed away. At first I couldn't believe the news; I couldn't. How could this possibly be true? Someone had to have made a mistake on the name. I've known Jennifer my whole life, she can't be gone; dear God please don't let this be true! I called Mark and left a message on his voicemail begging him to call me back and say it was a false report and everything was fine. I then called my dad, who then called the Paulson's......

Then it was confirmed: Jennifer was gone. I felt nauseated and shocked; I had to sit down and collect my thoughts. Of all the people this world needed, it was Jennifer. She didn't deserve this. My thoughts immediately went to her parents, and the horror they must have been facing at that moment. My heart went out to her brothers: Mark and Jason, because I knew they needed their sister. I considered her friends, Joellen and Jessica and the many others with whom she shared her life, because I knew they would be torn apart. Jennifer meant the world to all who knew her, and this world would not be the same without her.

I forced myself to get back to work and continue with my day. I fought back emotions and pain I never knew a human could feel. I felt devastation, anger, heartbreak, regret and grief, but at the same I felt pride, inspiration, joy and serenity because I had known Jennifer Ann Paulson. My life was changed because of who she was and Who she lived for. She was in heaven and I knew that above all else. I was excited for her: welcome home Jennifer!

GOD WAS WORKING

The next few days, as you can imagine, were extremely difficult for Jennifer's friends and family. The media had Jennifer's face on every local news station explaining again what had happened. They used the same words over and over again: murder, stalker, slain and violence. The local newspaper plastered Jennifer's face on the front page. The article was actually a very nice tribute to Jennifer but still difficult to read. All this attention made it even more surreal for her loved ones. But through it all God was working.

It is an amazing thing when tragedy strikes; all who mourn are drawn together with a common bond. Calls and letters are received from old friends. Old grudges seem to dissolve in the face of pain and suffering. What we held onto with our pride just doesn't seem all that important. The time of pain brings family and friends together. Our lives are going so fast and in so many directions, those who are most important to us are sometimes left in the dust. In times like this we find we need them more than ever, to help us grieve.

HOLY GROUND

The following Tuesday was the day Jennifer Ann Paulson would be laid to rest. Her life on this earth would be celebrated and her grave site would be a constant connection between heaven and earth. Yet this was not the end for Jennifer.

At 10 o'clock in the morning on March 2, 2010, friends and family gathered around the place where Jennifer's earthly body would return to dust. Tears flowed down the cheeks of those who loved her most as they tried to wrap their minds around the reality of what was happening. As Jennifer's brothers, step-brothers and cousins carried Jennifer's beautiful white and pink coffin from the hearse to the grave where her body would take residence, reality hit even harder.

The graveside ceremony is important in the process of grief, as well as the memorial service. These services take place in every city, every day all across the world. People come and go in the blink of an eye and grief is part of the human condition. But this graveside was special: we were on holy ground. It was the ground where a faithful follower of Jesus Christ was laid to rest.

As Dean Curry, the Senior Pastor of Life Center, began to share from God's Word, the Spirit of the living God descended on all those present. The Bible says the Holy Spirit is our comforter; and that day He surely was. He touched every heart and whispered to every ear words of peace and words of hope.

As the ceremony concluded and Jennifer's earthly body was about to be lowered into the ground, I realized someone was missing: it was Jennifer. I remember looking at her coffin and thinking to myself: it is just an empty box. Jennifer is not here today. She truly is alive and with God in a place we cannot even fathom or dream about, but we believe exists.

NO LONGER UNDER TIME'S CONTROL

As the ceremony came to a close, all in attendance recited the Lord's Prayer. The voices seemed to echo with the power behind them. We were all there in one accord, everyone sharing the same spirit.

Our Father, Who art in Heaven;
hallowed be Thy name.
Thy kingdom come,
Thy will be done on,
in earth as it is in heaven.
Give us this day our daily bread.
And forgive us our trespasses,
as we for give those who trespass against us.
And lead us not into temptation,
but deliver us from evil.
For Thine is the kingdom,
and the power and the glory
forever and ever,
Amen.

I have said this prayer hundreds of times in my life. So much that it almost has no meaning. I speak the words in church and never think about what they mean; but on this Tuesday morning this prayer was different.

As the prayer echoed across the grounds of that cemetery, as everyone in attendance said those words in one accord; the voices mired in grief, pain, heartache and anger. Each individual with their own emotions spoke the words Jesus taught us to pray. It was as if time disappeared and we were with Jesus in eternity. The word of the Lord is not bound by the clock. It has the same power today as it did the first time it was spoken.

Jennifer Ann Paulson is no longer under time's control. She has no beginning and no end. She has been reunited with her Grandparents who she missed so terribly. She now has the joy of being with a sibling who she had never met from her mother's miscarriage many years ago. She has been introduced to every spirit that has accepted salvation throughout history; each one of them having met death with the forgiveness of Christ in their hearts. Jennifer Ann Paulson fulfilled God's plan; she followed her map precisely and found the treasure. Eternity is now her timetable; forever and ever in the presence of God.

TIME TO CELEBRATE

Later that day, friends and family gathered at Life Center Assemblies of God to celebrate Jennifer's life. The clouds in the sky were beginning to scatter as morning turned to afternoon. It seemed fitting that after a grievous graveside service, the sun would begin to shine on the day, turning the mood slightly more optimistic.

Before the celebration began, those who were close to Jennifer and her family gathered in the chapel directly off of the main foyer. They rested, prayed and embraced as the reality of Jennifer's passing became more and more real. The celebration was streamed live on the internet for the community to view and is still available (http://www.kirotv.com/video/22745687/index.html), so there was a bit of an uneasy mood of the room, but nevertheless the same Holy Spirit, the same comforter, was in the midst of the people.

People from all over filled the sanctuary and extra chairs needed to be brought in to accommodate every one who came to pay their respects. As the family filed into the sanctuary every man woman and child stood in silence, in honor and in support. There was not a heart that was not touched by this show of affection.

As the service began, a picture of Jennifer was projected upon each wall. Her chin sat in her hand as she flashed that big smile. It seemed as if Jennifer was looking directly at each individual present that day, encouraging them to follow in her footsteps. The look on her face was not the picture of death, but a picture of life.

The celebration went on with Ken, Nancy, Cindy and Ned sharing hilarious and heartwarming stories of their daughter. Jennifer's pal, Joellen, and her brother Mark shared from their hearts as well. There was not a dry eye in the place as people realized how much Jennifer meant to her family and community.

Although these were the hardest days for Jennifer's parents, never once did they shake their fists toward heaven and curse God for not preventing Jennifer's death. On the contrary, they lifted their hands and hearts in faith, praising the Lord that Jennifer had salvation and that she was in heaven now. They never pointed fingers at the young man responsible or at his family. In fact, they stated publicly that they place no blame on his family but that they will pray for them; that they will find the peace they have.

As the celebration service came to a close, Dean Curry, Life Center's Senior Pastor shared these powerful final words in one sentence: *"The girl is the message!"* The life of Jennifer was God's living word. If ever anyone needed an example of a transparent and real Christian life, she was the example. She was the message the world needed, because she carried His message in her heart.

LIFE MUST GO ON

Time has marched on for those who loved Jennifer and still, she is gone. The grief has settled in and everyday can be a battle to overcome. Yes, there is faith and yes there is hope, but in the end the human heart still grieves. It is only natural. Jennifer's parents, brothers and friends have gone back to their everyday lives, and live as best they can, but with a heavy heart. The memories of Jennifer are all they have left. There is no way to say goodbye, or send a message to her expressing their pain. Things have to be laid to rest just the way they are. Jennifer left this world suddenly and unexpectedly. Whatever last words were spoken to her by those she cared about will have to remain as they are. They grief and sorrow may never subside – but life goes on.

It is through all this that God shows His face. A different perspective on life is adopted as we make sense of this. Our lives on this earth are so short in comparison to eternity. Each person is here and appointed by God to follow a certain course, and we each have a map to follow. No matter who you are, or where your life has taken you, God has a purpose. Each and every one of us must die to this world and we do not know when that will be. It is up to us to accept the forgiveness that Jesus offers and seek our purpose. He calls, but we must take the first steps. Because in the end, after our time for death comes and this earth withers away into dust, it will not matter how we died. But it will matter how we lived.

ONLY THE BEGINNING

Jennifer Ann Paulson was truly sold out to God's calling. Her heart was filled with faith and at the moment of her death, all that could save her was her faith. It did save her, and it can save you. Remember, dear reader, the life of Jennifer Paulson. Remember the pact she made as a child to be a missionary. Remember the girl who played the violin for the entire community. Remember the girl who stayed pure throughout her life, waiting for the man God had for her. Remember the girl who reached out to those no one would accept. Remember the girl with a spray painted car. Remember the girl that locked her brother out of the house when bees chased him. Remember the girl who lived her entire life for God, and let's live for God too. So that when our time comes and death comes for us, those who loved us most will remember and speak of us, as a life well lived.

EPILOGUE

When tragedy strikes its painful chord too close to home, our lives become uprooted and our hearts burn with grief. The loss of a loved one can feel nearly impossible to survive. As we attempt to pick up the broken pieces that are left of our lives, sift through the sands of devastation and move on, we find a hope that is ever enduring. That hope is in Jesus.

As that young man pulled that trigger and fled from the scene, Jennifer fell to the ground and breathed her last breath. I have often wondered since that day: what was Jennifer's last thought as she passed into eternity? Did her life pass before her eyes? If so, what did she see? I guarantee she had not one regret. Her heart was pure and a beautiful act of worship to the One who has now given her a new life and a new home. Jennifer is with her Savior now. She is at peace, and she is very much alive.

Jennifer's life was not stolen that Friday morning. She was not robbed of a future that she so desperately deserved; it was just her time to go home. A bullet did not claim her life; it merely set her free from the burden of humanity. She is separated from the frailty of flesh and now lives life as God truly designed it to be lived – a life she wants each and every one of us to experience. It was Jennifer's passion for the Lord that led her down life's road with an unwavering passion for people. The Lord gave her His eyes to see people as He saw them: full of potential and value. She looked beyond the superficial value of a person, and saw their heart and destiny.

Police officers gave chase to the young man who took Jennifer's life. As they caught up to him thirty minutes later and that young man also met his death, I wonder what was going through his mind. Was he sorry for what he did? Did he feel guilt and fear? We may never know, but one thing is certain: Jennifer prayed for that young man, that he would find Jesus; and maybe before he died, he did.

The time came for Jennifer, as it will for every one of us who follow Christ like Jennifer did. We will be separated from our earthly bodies and be reunited with our loved ones who have gone on before us. But *we* have to choose Christ; no one can choose for us. We each need to ask Jesus to forgive our sins and admit that we were wrong. Jennifer made that choice and walked the road less traveled despite the opposition that life threw in on her. At the end of that road, in the early morning of February 26, 2010, she was not murdered, Jesus called her home. Her mission was complete and her reward was great.

As her hand went to her wound and she fell to the ground; her body shut down, but Jennifer did not. Jesus came to her, picked her up, and carried her in His strong arms to the gates of heaven and placed her down to be greeted by all those who had gone on before her – and what a reception it must have been. Jesus then led her to the feet of the Almighty God, and He greeted her with those words all His followers long to hear: *"Well done, my good and faithful servant."*

So, you see dear reader, the story of Jennifer Ann Paulson has not ended, it has only just begun. She will live on in her legacy – laughter, memory, joy and tears. We must remember that all our days are pre-ordained, and that each day we wake up, we are one day closer to being in heaven with her again. For when that day comes, she will be there to greet us, and grief and sorrow will be no more....

Questions for Discussion:

1. In your own circle of influence, who could you be reaching out to that may need a friend?

2. What are you/ or have you been doing to prepare for God's calling in your own life?

3. Jennifer's Grandparents set the stage for who she would become. Who in your life has set the stage?

4. How are you setting the stage for those who follow you?

5. In what ways are the characteristics of Christ showing in your life?

6. How will you be remembered?

7. If you were to die today, would you be with the Lord in heaven? What is your assurance?

8. Do you feel you have a clear vision of what God wants to do in your life?

Acknowledgments

There are so many to thank for helping me bring Jennifer's life to written word. First off, I would like to thank Jennifer's parents and brothers for trusting me with her life and reputation. I also thank her dear, dear friends, Joellen, Jessica, Colleen, Sarah, Jenniey, Rochelle, and Jill for all of the memories and laughter you shared with me- I hope I did them justice. Thank you to Chris Hinds, Ann Smith and Deborah Raynes of the Tacoma School District. Thank you to my lovely wife Naomi for your love and support during this entire project; and for sleeping through the sound of typing as I burned the midnight oil. Thank you to my own mother, Margaret Lundberg, for your brilliant editing. Thank you, Pastor Nils and Pat Leksen for your constant encouragement. Thank you, Pastor Dean Curry and Heather Schmick of Life Center. Thank you to Rob Restowitz of Urban Promise Ministries. Thank you to Stan Seeley. I want also to thank Yvonne Olson and Kris M. Smith for their instruction in the craft of writing. Thank you to Laurine Decker for the beautiful picture on the cover. Also, I would like to acknowledge the music of Addison Road for inspiring me through my tough bouts with writers block and Steven Curtis Chapman's album written for his baby girl, which allowed me a glimpse into a parent's soul.

.........And of course, to Jennifer Ann Paulson for living her life in God's eye's and leaving behind a legacy that will live on through our children and our children's children.